J O A N A   I N C H

GO TO
MARKET

The marketing and scaling
blueprint for startups

R^ethink

To all my best teachers in life:
Romi, George, Vlady, Nigel and Dave

Contents

Introduction

Born and raised in 1950s Bulgaria during a communist era that imposed many limitations, my parents looked for a way out. With one suitcase packed and two small children, they took their engineering degrees and fled.

The first stop was Baghdad, Iraq, where construction was booming under Saddam Hussein's rule. They struggled with the heat, the language and the culture shock but were not deterred by their two-year stay. My dad settled in fine. My mum was an engineer going to work in a man's world, where as a woman she was expected to wear particular attire and definitely no pants were allowed. Despite the paradigm shift, she was treated well and they made good money and good friends, and learned new skills, which gave them the opportunity to apply for a visa to their real country of choice – Australia.

An engineer's dream? My dad, a civil engineer, has told me how his school classrooms were covered in posters of the Sydney Opera House and Sydney Harbour Bridge and how he dreamt to see such unique constructions in real life. But what to do while waiting for this visa to be approved? He couldn't stay in Bulgaria, didn't want to stay in Iraq.

Next stop – Rome, Italy, and at last their youngest child (me) was finally of school age so they could catch a bit of a break. The air was sweet and smelled of gaming arcades and margarita pizza or *Pizza Rossa*. At least, that's how I remember it as a six-year-old. I'm sure it was different for them. This destination was short-lived and lasted only six months as word came that they had finally received their visas for Australia.

Excitedly, we packed what little we had in one car and sped towards the border to say *dovishdane* to our family in Bulgaria. But first, another hurdle. The car was stopped at the border in Italy. No, we were told, we cannot keep driving, not today and not for another few months – they have to keep the car as it's unregistered and must be inspected. *What do we do?* we thought. *Australia is calling.*

We abandoned the car and took the train. I couldn't take any of my luggage – there was no car to carry it.

I remember having to leave behind my favourite toy (a little plastic washing machine that I pretended to wash my doll's clothes in) but I don't remember the train trip that took us through the civil war that Serbia and Croatia were engaged in at the time. Our journey saw us pull over at what wouldn't be considered the safest of stops, considering all the soldiers and weapons around us at the time. Amazing how the brain works at forgetting certain information and protecting oneself. That toy, though…

We finally got on the longest flight of my life. Thirty-six hours later we landed in Sydney, Australia, and my dad exclaimed, 'Oops, wrong country.'

I'm sure you remember the recession of the early 1990s. When jobs were lost, unemployment rates reached 17% and so did interest rates. It was 1992. Nobody was funding construction at that time, and nobody was hiring new immigrant engineers either. Although their visa had been approved due to their engineering qualifications and experience, that now seemed completely irrelevant.

Wanting to give it a chance for at least a year, they made a home and opted for whatever work they could find. Pizza delivery driver, salesperson, drafter – nothing was beneath them. They just wanted to make it work. Twenty-eight years later, here they still are, now officially retired and living their best life.

What's the learning of this story? It shows how many hurdles my parents had to overcome to achieve their dream and get to where they are. Their perseverance is what helped them succeed.

As a startup, you're going to come up against many hurdles yourself, and how you deal with them will determine your success. I've seen this with many of my clients and I'll share their stories in later chapters. If you can persevere and get past all the obstacles that come your way, I'm sure you'll reach your destination. I'm just here to help make your journey easier.

This book is not about making you more resilient – there are lots of other books on that topic, my personal favourite being *The Obstacle is the Way* by Ryan Holiday. This book is about best practices for taking your product to market. The fun part.

Once you've gone through the creative process and you have your minimal viable product (MVP), what do you do next? How do you take the leap and start making money from it? Fifteen years in the world of digital marketing and fifteen years of helping small businesses and startups scale up has taught me many lessons, which I'm sharing with you in this book.

I founded my own startup, Hat Media, a digital marketing agency, to focus specifically on helping technology and software companies scale and grow. Now a mature adult at ten years of age, it has allowed me to work on many inspiring projects and achieve so much. I was nominated for a Women in Media award by B&T when I was thirty years old. It set me on the path towards helping women in tech. The company saw some nominations too, for Best Content & Best Collaboration by Mumbrella Asia. We also have the following results to our name:

- We helped tech giant Lenovo earn US$66 million in twelve months from content marketing.

- We helped Dell EMC bring their annual forum to an online platform.

- We helped Navman Wireless increase their lead generation results by 975%.

- My team played a crucial role in this success and if there's one thing I've always known and said in life, it's that you need to surround yourself with great, positive minds. People who you can learn from.

We worked with many enterprise clients, not just in Australia but globally. As we did more projects for these conglomerates, I realised that my true passion and calling lies with helping the startup community instead, because this is where I can make a real difference. This is where we can innovate and introduce a new and exciting idea. It's where we can do our best work that can truly change the world and make it a better place.

I have helped many startups scale and grow, but my favourite so far has been QSN Health, a small, Australia-based company that helps people quit smoking. Here were two founders with one amazing product that truly works. It was tear-jerking watching the stories of their customers as they won their battle against cigarettes. Calling these people 'overjoyed' would be an understatement. Theirs are by far the most rewarding customer success stories we have ever filmed.

QSN Health has come a long way. They are now five years old, have helped over 21,000 people quit smoking and have expanded to include a holistic wellness package. Our next mission and journey for them? Go global and help one million people quit smoking. How exciting!

I love helping startups because this is where the best ideas are born and it's so exciting bringing them to the world and making it a better place. Just look at some of the most successful startups that were born during a recession, like Uber and Airbnb. The ways they have changed the world we live in is phenomenal.

I believe you can make a difference also. This book is here to give you the blueprint to do just that.

SECTION 1

BUILD YOUR FOUNDATION

Building your foundation is crucial to any successful marketing campaign. Fail at this initial phase and you will have a hard time scaling your business. Think of it like building a house. Adding the rooms and interior is the fun part, where you get the most recognition. But if you hadn't laid that slab of concrete deep in the ground to support the structure and the rooms then your house would not have survived long enough to be decorated.

Not only that but you wouldn't be able to build any rooms on top. There would be no opportunities for expansion (or scaling in your business). Because everything on top relies on the stability and success of that below it. That's why you need an engineer to help build the foundations of your house, well before you give the work to a builder to complete the finishings and make it look good. In case you haven't guessed, the builder in my analogy would be your marketing campaigns that you create to scale your business, and the engineer is you. You're the person responsible for the foundation because nobody knows your business better than you. Sure, marketing experts can help get you there, but you need to be significantly involved in this step. If you don't have your building blocks nailed, then you will have the whole structure topple on top of you with thousands of dollars down the drain.

That's where most founders and marketers fail. They believe they can skip this step. Founders either assume they know their target audience well because they've walked in their shoes and so do little research on them; or they believe they need as many customers as possible and cast too wide a net to fish with. But being many things to many people is not effective. Casting a wide net may get you fish but it will also get you some junk and then you'll have to waste time sorting through it. In this time, your fish could swim away. You'll end up losing a good client because your focus was not on point and you didn't spend your time wisely.

It's not about quantity when you need to scale. You need to catch the right customers who will form the right success stories and help set more foundations for you to scale from. Many times over, companies get bogged down in servicing the wrong customers – those who are never happy and always want more for less. By finding and securing the right customers, you avoid all that time-wasting and instead focus your energy on growing your company and providing the right services.

For marketers, they've likely been asked to come in after a few years of the startup growing. Their challenge is to keep that growth-rate going. It's typical of startups to grow fast at the beginning, especially if they have formed good networks or partnerships with the right people and if they have created something great, but they always reach that revenue plateau. That's usually when they hire the marketing expert to come in and help them scale.

The biggest mistake I've seen marketers make at this stage is to attempt to launch big-budget advertising campaigns without looking at the foundations. You need to refresh and revise your foundations at every growth phase your business is experiencing if you want to move past the plateau.

It's likely your niche will have changed and so your message will need to also. You'll need to examine the entire structure, starting with the roof and walls (your messages) and then observe your stormwater drainage (content strategy) to ensure the structure is getting the right results. If not, and if inbound marketing efforts have been disappointing, then more than likely the house (the foundation) has not been maintained properly. In this case, you'll need to start from scratch.

Do a 'buyer persona' workshop with the entire team. Get as many team members on board as possible for this one. Especially those who speak to customers on a regular basis, like the sales team and customer support team. Spend half a day in a room together asking all the right questions (provided for you in Chapter 1 – 'Nailing Your Niche'). The objective is to fully understand who your market is, what their pain points are, what keeps them up at night and how you can help them solve this. Once you have this nailed, the rest is easy. You'll understand how to speak to them and create the right content for them with the right tools, as you'll know exactly who they are.

You may find me using construction analogies in this book quite a bit. It comes from a good place. I grew up in a family of engineers and I even ended up marrying one. It seemed to be my destiny. I call myself a 'marketing engineer'. I like to break down marketing plans to identify the blueprint as well as the strategies designed not only to hold the structure up safely and securely but to allow the business to expand and scale.

The sky's the limit. I will show you some of these blueprints and strategies in the following chapters.

1

Nailing Your Niche

O ver my fifteen-year career in digital marketing, I have worked with many well-known enterprise clients in the tech and SaaS space. My true passion, though, comes from helping startups. They are not limited by legal teams going over every bit of content and slowing things down and there is so much opportunity to be creative and scale. If you're reading this and working in a startup right now, I know you have a wonderful career ahead of you, full of so many exciting opportunities.

But among all of these clients, whether they be enterprise or startup, I see many of them struggling to define their niche. Startups tend to try and target everybody and acquire as many customers as they can, with many not being the right type of customer, which actually hurts their scaling process. Enterprises have often evolved so much over the years that their niche has changed and they haven't adapted yet. They are still sending the same messages targeting the same people when in actual fact, that audience is different.

Keep in mind that you're not thinking small by having a niche, you're actually becoming laser-focused on a specific customer with a specific need. This focus will significantly help you scale.

Defining your niche

Why is it so crucial that you nail your niche? Well, if you don't completely understand your niche, then you can't run your most effective marketing campaign. Why? Because you're trying to be many things to many people and are likely sending out conflicting messages that don't appeal to any specific audience. Your message needs clarification and doesn't resonate with your primary buyer persona, let alone your secondary one.

Before you can clarify your message (which I talk you through in the next chapter), you really need to have nailed your niche. This means you need to learn more about your customers. Don't fret – I have a list of questions for you to answer to help you do just that, inspired by the book *From Impossible to Inevitable: How*

SaaS and other hyper-growth companies create predictable revenue by Aaron Ross and Jason Lemkin, the VC and founder of SaaStr.

How do you nail your niche?

The first step is to answer the following questions:

- What pain points are you trying to solve?

- How are you making your customers' lives better?

- What are your proven results?

- Where have you achieved your best results?

- What common problem have you built a reputation for solving?

Let's look more in-depth at this to help you determine your exact niche. Answer the following questions:

- What are your top four projects that you've worked on? List your best projects, both in terms of the ones you found most enjoyable as well as where you achieved an impressive result. Considering you are a startup and may not have customers on board just yet, the idea here is to reflect back on your previous career, if relevant, or your dream projects if not.

- Now describe the product or service you are selling. What is your 'elevator pitch'? Is it related to the projects you listed above? Does it have the same target audience?

- What is the problem that your product fixes? Here, you want to be able to demonstrate to your niche that you understand what their typical problems and issues are. If you know this well, then you know your niche and you can then describe the solution for them.

- What impressive results did you achieve from these projects?

- What was your ROI for each project?

- On a scale of 1 to 10, with 1 being very difficult and 10 being very easy, how easy would it be for you to scale if you only worked on projects like the ones you have listed?

- Detail the special features and benefits your product has over your competition.

- If people purchased your product for just one thing, what would it be? Can you productise this benefit to a specific niche?

Are you starting to see a pattern emerge? These questions should give you a good indication not just of where your passion lies and what problems you love to solve but also of which ones make you more money and give you the opportunity to scale. We can't work for love forever. You'll have to productise that love at some point or the business will be unsustainable.

Indications you haven't nailed your niche

If you're going to sales meetings and getting asked, 'What do I get, and what have you done for my industry?' and you're coming up short on those answers, then you know you haven't nailed your niche. It's cases like these that prevent you from scaling as quickly as you would like. You have an asset deficiency, which you need to rectify to prove to this potential client that you can do a good job.

But let's say you spend time creating that and you spend time in countless more meetings, only to be told that they've gone with a competitor that specialises in their particular industry. If you had focused on one niche, you would have had proven results and an abundance of assets and content to share with your client in that same niche. It would have been quick and easy to send them the data they were seeking, and the deal would likely have gone in your favour as a result.

Here are some more subtle signs that you haven't nailed your niche:

- **You've grown mostly through your existing network and their friends** – As luck would have it, you know some pretty cool people who happen to want to use your software and you have a great network that you can tap into. Your software also happens to be quite good so those people have told their network of friends.

Well done! You've got your first batch of Annual Recurring Revenue (ARR) that can now sustain you. But you can't rely on this method for further growth and hyper-growth. This will reach a plateau at some point, so you need to expand your reach. This can only be done via partnerships and marketing.

If you haven't done any marketing to date and have just relied on referrals then it's likely you don't know too much about your niche. Before you start any marketing activities, be sure to talk to your existing customers and answer the questions under 'How to nail your niche' so that you can determine who your optimum customer is.

- **Your lead generation efforts have been discouraging** – Usually this is the case if you haven't nailed your niche. Why? You're not targeting the right people and therefore you're not using the right messages. It's likely you're trying to be too many things to too many people, with generic, non-customer-centric messages, which is why you're getting few sales and conversions.

- **Even when you do get quality leads, they don't turn into customers** – The reason for this is the asset deficiency I spoke about earlier. It is likely that you don't have proven results for that industry or for that customer persona because they are not in your niche. Your competitors may have those assets because they have been around longer and have focused on that niche – that's why you're missing out on that sale.

Evolving your niche

It is crucial that you keep revisiting the questions about your niche and evolving it as you grow. Why? Because you'll also keep growing and changing. You can – and should – develop more niches as you develop more products and services.

You may add new products and features. Your customers may change themselves and be instrumental in changing your software by motivating you to add more features specifically for them. You may be smart enough to keep up with innovation and add new tools and technologies yourself. Your marketing efforts and company culture may earn you a certain reputation, which would also change your niche.

It is likely you have more than one niche. If this is true for your business, you need to determine which product belongs to which niche, nail all your niches and divide your marketing messaging to focus on each relevant niche.

There are some great examples of this among some of the best-known tech companies:

- Facebook began with Ivy League schools and then opened to everyone. It continues to be the most used platform across the globe to date.

- PayPal took off with eBay users and now it's accepted across most online shopping websites across the globe.

- Amazon started out with books and now look at them. You simply have to view a YouTube video of how their supply chain works and go, *'Wow, when did we enter the future!'*

So you see, having a niche does not limit you. It allows you to be laser-focused and cater specifically to one particular audience. This in turn allows you to build success and a reputation, to scale more easily and quickly. Once you scale, you'll recruit more assets, people and technology to help you cater to your new clientele, allowing you to further expand and discover new products or niches you can work with.

In his studies of the natural world, Darwin observed that it wasn't the strongest members of the species, nor the cleverest, who were more likely to survive – it was those who were most adaptable to change. The same goes in the world of business. Keep evolving, because life is supposed to evolve.

2

Clarify Your Message

Once you've nailed your niche and you know exactly who your customer is, the next step is to determine how are you going to speak to them at each step of the journey, from the top to the bottom of the funnel.

Writing customer-centric copy

Your message needs to answer three important questions at first glance:

1. What do you offer?

2. How can it help me?

3. How do I buy it?

All three need to be answered in your customer's language. Not yours. Avoid using jargon and talking about your product's features and benefits. Focus instead on your customer's biggest concerns, pain points and desires.

The best way to do this is by engaging in a little exercise I like to call 'Inner versus Outer'. As you know, your message needs to solve your customer's pain points so that they feel like you actually understand them and can help them.

Inner versus outer

What's the difference between inner and outer problems?

- Outer problems are problems that you'd *like* to solve.

- Inner problems are problems that you *need* to solve.

- Outer problems challenge you to think.

- Inner problems keep you up at night, stressed.

- Outer problems are easy to solve as you can think through them logically.

- Inner problems are hard to solve as you're too emotional or close to the problem to be able to think clearly about the solution.

If you can solve your customers' outer problems, so can a handful of your competitors and it's likely they are using messaging on their website that is targeted towards them.

If you can solve your customers' inner problems, you win the game. They will go with you because they can breathe a sigh of relief. Let's look at an example.

If you were a standard car company called Car Company XYZ and you were selling based on your customers' outer problems, you would say something like this: 'View the entire XYZ range, access latest offers, find service information and locate your nearest dealer.'

There is no emotion. As a customer, I'm thinking, 'Just a car that gets me from A to B.' As you can see, it's focused on the company, their range, their latest offers, their service information and their location. It's all about them solving your outer problem of needing a car.

What if they were to focus on your inner problem? On your right and desire for freedom and mobility, comfort for your family or your need for the security and safety of your family. Wouldn't that be a much better sell? You bet it would.

Take a look at Tesla in comparison. What's their message? 'Lay rubber where your carbon footprint used to be.'

Their mission statement: 'To accelerate the advent of sustainable transport.'

By touching on environmental problems, they trigger an inner concern and fear that we have about the world. This message focuses on a desire that most people have: to be better, to do better.

If I were to look at your company's current messaging, your website copy and other content assets that you use to describe what you do, what would I find? Are you talking about yourself or are you talking with the customer in mind? Are you solving their outer problems or inner problems?

I challenge you to step into your customers' shoes. Identify what their inner problems are. Then think about how your product can improve their lives. You'll need to think outside the box here, so the last thing you should do is visit competitor websites and try to be like them. Instead, really think about how *your* message can help them feel at ease and breathe that sigh of relief that they have finally found a solution to their problem. Touch on your customers' pain points and desires in your message and you'll have a clear winner.

Compassion and influence

There are two more factors that you need to consider when clarifying your company message. The first is compassion. This means you should write in a way that makes your customer believe you understand their problem. When your messaging is compassionate, it has a customer-centric philosophy. And when you make it all about them instead of you, guess what? You'll come out on top.

The second thing is influence. It's great if you understand your customers and you know how to solve their problems, but they won't buy from you unless you're able to show your influence in the space and industry you work in. How do you do this? By including testimonials, reviews, customer success stories and statistics in your messaging.

Capturing conversions

We've looked at how your message answers 'what do you offer?' and 'how can it help me?'. Now we want to answer: 'How do I buy it?'

You'd be surprised how many websites I've seen where I've wanted to buy but the journey has been so difficult. I knew what they were selling. I knew it would make my life easier. I wanted to buy it. But the call to action just wasn't there. One made me click three or four times before I could find what I wanted, which left me with such a bad customer experience, I didn't buy from them.

It's really important to make your call to action prominent, and for it to appear at the top of your website. Let's take a look at this website wireframe to show you what I mean.

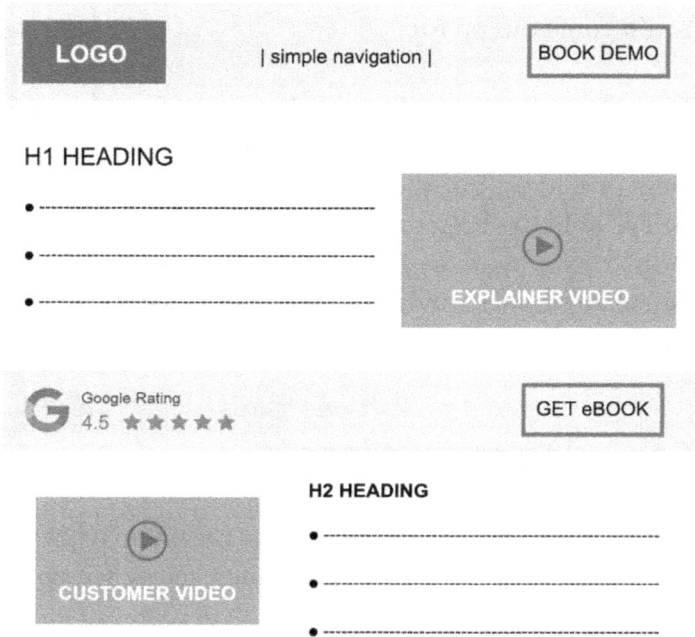

| LOGO | | simple navigation | | BOOK DEMO |

H1 HEADING

- ------------------------------------
- ------------------------------------
- ------------------------------------

EXPLAINER VIDEO

Google Rating
4.5 ★★★★★

GET eBOOK

CUSTOMER VIDEO

H2 HEADING

- ------------------------------------
- ------------------------------------
- ------------------------------------

Example of a website wireframe

If you look closely, you'll notice there are two crucial calls to action on the website. The first is the direct one: 'Book demo'. On your site, this should be the main call to action you want people to click on – 'book a demo', 'book a quick chat' or 'schedule a meeting', for example. It is prominent on the top right side of the website where people expect it to be. Make sure you make it a different colour from the rest of the navigation menu, and if you can also have that navigation menu follow website visitors down as they're scrolling, then you're already winning.

Not all website visitors are ready to make that commitment on first visit, though, so what you also need to provide is an intermediate call to action. Here, it's 'Get eBook', but for you it might be 'register for our webinar', 'take our quiz', 'sign up for our newsletter' – whatever secondary action you would like your customers to take. This can be placed at the bottom of the section 'above the fold' on your website, ie the portion of the webpage that is visible without scrolling.

This acts as a value offer and enables you to capture their contact details and continue to nurture them further down the marketing funnel. We'll look more at lead nurturing and marketing automation in later chapters.

The importance of position

You'll see that all the important elements are included 'above the fold', so on first look the customer already knows what you're about and how you serve to benefit them. They've also scanned your reviews and customer success stories without having to scroll much, so they quickly feel like you have the authority to help them and keep reading.

I've also positioned the 'influence' element of the website not just above the fold but also strategically near the calls to action. It includes a customer success story video and a Google rating, which create authority. In my experience, having these elements near the call-to-action buttons creates more conversions.

Keep navigation simple

You'll notice I've included a simple navigation menu. My recommendation here is to keep this as minimal as possible and add all your other pages in the footer.

I can't tell you how many video recordings of people browsing websites I've watched in my life (more than a thousand for sure) and I always see the same pattern on websites that have too much going on in the navigation menu. Visitors get extremely overwhelmed with the choices and either go on a clicking frenzy, leading down a rabbit hole, or they scroll down to get away from it and then jump off the site. Try to keep your customer's journey on your website simple and give them an easy path to follow.

Make your copy work for your customer

The copy that I've included in the wireframe is labelled H1, then body copy, H2, then more body copy. Not only is this a structure that improves Search Engine Optimisation factors but it's also visually appealing.

It also encompasses a video and summarised text in bullet points because in this day and age, let's face it, people want to know what you do and how it serves them quickly. Pronto, snap, now. *Don't waste my time.* Don't expect them to read a ton of text to discover what you do. They'll get overwhelmed at the sight of it and quickly leave your site. Keep it simple and offer both a visual explanation as well as one they can read.

Your website doesn't have to look exactly like this one to be effective, but if you can follow the majority of these simple best practices, it will serve you well.

EXERCISE: WRITING CUSTOMER-CENTRIC COPY

This exercise will significantly help you write customer-centric copy on your website and other content assets. Get your pen and paper out and really spend some time considering the following questions.

- Can you identify the main problem that your customer faces?
- What is a problem your customers deal with relating to your product or service?
- What challenges are you helping your customers overcome?
- Next, consider the answers to the above questions in light of the four categories below.
- **Emotion** – How is this problem making your customers feel? What keeps them up at night? What consumes them emotionally, that you can solve?

- **Compassion** – What messages can you write about your product that expresses empathy with your customer's problems? Have you walked in their shoes and developed this product to help others like you?

- **Influence** – How can you demonstrate your competency for solving your customer's problem? What influence do you have in the industry? Think about customer success stories, partnerships, results, your professional experience.

- **Action** – What is your direct call to action and where does it appear on your customer's buying journey? What is your intermediate call to action and where does that appear on their journey?

If you struggle with completing this exercise, you may want to speak to existing customers to understand more about their problems and customer buying experience, as understanding this will help you immensely.

Remember, the clearer you are about what you want, the more likely you are to achieve it.

3

Mapping Your Buyer Journey

OK, you've nailed your niche, you know who you're going to target and you know what you're going to say to them. The next step is mapping out your buyer journey.

The buyer journey map

A buyer journey map is a visual representation of every stage where your customer engages with your company or product, from their first interaction with your brand to after they have purchased from you.

First of all, don't feel like you need to create a visually stunning chart. It doesn't have to be beautiful. It just needs to be functional and has to make sense to you (and your marketing team). If you're anything like me, you'll prefer to work in a spreadsheet.

Here's an example of a spreadsheet you can get started with.

The Journey	Awareness	Consideration	Decision	Customer
Pain point				
Touchpoint				
Call to action				
Content type				
Emotion				
Data gathering				
Goal				
Key metric				

The journey sample spreadsheet

Let's look at what you can do at each part of the buyer journey, as the buyer moves from awareness of your product to consideration of it, decision to buy, and, finally, purchasing the product – becoming a customer.

Pain points

The journey that your customer takes starts with their awareness of your brand or product. In this phase, you need to make them aware of how your product can solve a pain point that they are experiencing. Remember the rules from Chapter 2 when filling this out. Don't focus on their outer problems and how your product or features work. Focus on their inner problems and how you can solve them and help them. Name the main pain points that your customers are experiencing at the awareness phase of their journey.

As they make their way further down the funnel, be sure to showcase ways in which you can solve these pain points and continue to reinforce your authority and influence so that they choose to work with you instead of a competitor. This is best done through the use of case studies, customer success stories and explainer videos or webinars.

I also recommend connecting with them on LinkedIn and reaching out with a message as well as a phone call so that you can start to build a relationship and they can put a face towards the brand. In the end, people prefer to buy from people, not from brands.

Touchpoint

Next, consider what touchpoint you will use for them to see your message. If your product is for consumers, you may use Google Search or Facebook ads. If your product is for businesses, you may consider LinkedIn Ads. If you're a startup, you'll likely have to advertise, so consider which channel will get you the best outcome for driving customer awareness.

As the customer makes their way across to the consideration and decision phase of the buyer journey, your touchpoints should change to remarketing ads and email marketing.

Call to action

You'll need to determine a suitable call to action for each of your platforms and touchpoints. Assume that your visitor is totally confused and does not know what actions you want them to take. Make it easy for them by telling them exactly what you want them to do. Communication is key.

Also consider what stage of their customer journey they are on as this will ensure they don't get scared away by being asked to take an action that they are not yet ready for. For example, not everyone is ready to book a demo now. Nor are they ready to book a 15-min consult with you. For those that are early on in their customer journey, you may just want them to learn more about your expertise first. Therefore, a more suitable call to action could be to download your guide or watch your webinar on a topic that would help to add value to their day.

Content type

Next, consider what content you will use to capture your audience's attention and, more importantly, their contact details, so you can continue to nurture the customer relationship. Will you write a blog or an eBook? Will you host a webinar? Or will you run sponsored ads with your key message? I recommend a combination of all of those – and remember to keep testing and measuring to find your sweet spot.

As your buyer moves from awareness of your product to consideration and decision making, your content type should change to case studies and customer success stories to encourage them to buy. And when they do, they'll reach the customer phase of the buyer journey and your content will change again – to information about the product or service, such as training videos.

Emotion

The emotion in the table above is what you want them to feel once they've read your content. In the awareness phase, do you want them to feel curious, overwhelmed or aware they are in need of help? Whatever emotion you pick, it needs to help get them to the next step – consideration of your product. The same goes for each subsequent stage of the journey.

Data gathering

Data gathering is crucial to any marketing campaign, at every stage. If you're putting out content to acquire new customers and keep them interested, you need to have a basic understanding of how this content is performing and resonating with them. What is the engagement score on your social channels? More importantly, what percentage of viewers are signing up for your content and providing you with contact details? And what is their satisfaction rating with your product?

You may like to use marketing automation software to capture all this information and run an automated report on it. For any busy founder that's head deep in all the requirements needed to go to market, I recommend an easy-to-use platform like HubSpot, which provides all the tools you need to get started for a monthly fee. (As an approved HubSpot for Startups Partner, Hat Media offers insights and education on this marketing automation platform for its startup community.) You can easily create forms that gather data such as name, email, phone number and (if you're in the b2b space) job title and company name.

I recommend asking for no more than four fields initially from your readers, otherwise they will get overwhelmed and simply log off. Adding a form like this on your website or landing page is a simple copy and paste job, and off you go!

Goal

You should also consider your main goal/s for gathering the data, and the key metrics you'll use to track these goals.

According to John Doerr, ex-Intel and Google visionary and bestselling author of *Measure What Matters*, the simple idea of implementing OKRs (Objectives and Key Results) can result in 10x growth for a company. Hence, it's crucial to set a goal or an objective. This can be something that you hope to achieve within the next three months. Some examples include:

- 100 webinar sign-ups

- $50k in Annual Recurring Revenue (ARR)

- 5 new Sales Qualified Leads (SQLs)

Ensure that your goal is a short-term goal. If you set yourself a goal that is three months away, you're more likely to stay focused on it and be able to quickly shift gears if needed in order to reach it.

If it's longer than three months, you'll likely lose track of it and you won't implement the necessary changes to your marketing campaigns quickly enough to ensure you're on track to reach it.

I always say to my clients that three months is a key measurement metric as any less means not enough data and any more means you're missing opportunities.

Once you've determined your main goal, you should then create a set of key metrics that you will use to measure if you're on track to reach it.

Key metrics

Key metrics help you stay focused on your goal. I recommend revisiting and updating the data on these every two weeks to ensure you're on track to meet your goal. Let's explore some common key metrics you can use.

If our goal was to close five Sales Qualified Leads (SQL) in three months, then we would work backwards and set the following key metrics:

- Number of Marketing Qualified Leads (MQLs) – may need 25 in 3 months in order to create 5 SQLs

- Number of leads – may need 100 leads in order to create 25 MQLs

- Number of contacts – may need 500 contacts in order to create 100 leads

- Number of website/landing page visits – may need 2,000 visits in order to create 500 contacts

Any marketing automation platform will allow you to create qualification criteria around these metrics and help you produce real-time dashboards to help you keep track of the numbers.

Over time, when you analyse the data, you will discover the exact percentages and numbers you need for each metric and hence be able to set more realistic goals based on solid data.

Measuring each metric will also allow you to determine where exactly you are struggling. Are you not generating enough contacts for example? If so, then we'll either need to adjust our expectations of this number or amend our marketing campaigns or content offers to help meet them.

Because we're viewing this data on a regular basis (every two weeks), we can quickly act to ensure we meet our main goal

Here is an example of a completed buyer journey map (at its briefest). In this example, my target audience is startups looking to go to market:

The Journey	Awareness	Consideration	Decision	Customer
Pain point	How do I launch my product and gain customers?	I know what to do but how do I do it right?	Let's do this! But who should I contact for a strategy to help me get started?	Is this really going to work?
Touchpoint	LinkedIn, Zoom	Remarketing, email, LinkedIn	Remarketing, email, LinkedIn	Weekly calls, live dashboards and reports
Call to action	Sign up for webinar	Book a strategy consultation	Book a strategy consultation	• Attend weekly Zoom calls • View reports
Content type	Webinar on go-to-market strategies	Blogs, email copy to further educate on go-to-market strategies	Case studies, email copy to sell strategy consultation	Personalised content strategy and monthly reports
Emotion	Overwhelmed	Curious	Optimistic	Happy with choice
Data gathering	Name, email, phone	Engagement data	Engagement data	Customer satisfaction data
Goal	Webinar sign-ups	Email engagement	Close customer	• Keep customer • Obtain referral
Key metric	• Impressions • Clicks • Sign-ups • Social engagement	• Email open rate • Email click rate	• Call details • Presentation details • Meeting obtained	• Call attendance • Happiness metric • Referral opportunities • Upsell opportunities

Sample completed buyer journey map

Eight tips for effective mapping

You can go to https://blog.hatmedia.com.au/buyer-journey-map to download a copy of your own map and get started. But before you do, I have eight crucial reminders that will help you complete this effectively, some of which we have touched on already.

Remember to:

1. Define your niche

2. Map out your key messages

3. Map out your direct and intermediate calls to action

4. Define channels and touchpoints

5. Explore your customers' pain points

6. Explore your customers' emotions

7. Use customer language

8. Add flexibility jumps

Using customer language is something I cannot emphasise enough. In my fifteen years in marketing and working with all types of clients, not using customer language is the one error I see time and time again. I see so much jargon on websites, especially software and tech websites, where they tend to focus on their features. You need to speak your customer's language if you want them to notice you and commit to you. You need to clarify what your product does for *them* in the most basic of ways so they are not burning brain cells trying to figure it out.

Flexibility jumps

Something we haven't yet touched upon is to add flexibility jumps. Understand that the buyer journey is not always linear. A person may not just go from A to B or from Awareness to Customer. They might have to go back a step or two due to all sorts of internal issues. Perhaps they have a contract with a competitor that needs to end first. Perhaps they've just been made redundant. Perhaps they've just had their budgets cut. Perhaps there's a pandemic that's forced everyone into lockdown. You just never know what could happen, but you should always prepare for something, which is where flexibility jumps come in.

What can potential flexibility jumps look like?

- You may have to move the person out of the existing email workflow and add them to a monthly newsletter list instead so that your brand is top of mind for when they are finally ready.

- You may consider offering a discount to people if you know their reasons for not converting are budget restrictions. For the same reason, you may want to add flexibility with the terms and contracts. Rather than twelve months, offer three months as a commitment option.

- You may have to re-engage with a new person in the same role and move them to the top of the funnel or to the start of the buyer journey once again.

Measure, test, optimise

Most importantly, ensure you are measuring everything. Use advertising platforms such as Google, Facebook and LinkedIn to measure conversion data. Use these same platforms to A/B test everything (more on this in Chapter 4) and ensure you're always optimising things like your ad copy, your targeting parameters, your placements and your touchpoints, as well as your content.

Determine how long the sales cycle is (you can use a marketing automation platform to do this) and what you can do to optimise it. The sales cycle refers to the length of time between first contact with an account/person to them becoming a customer. This is an important metric to know and measure if you want to build a stable business. A stable business should have a pipeline with contacts at all stages of their buyer journey and by understanding how long it takes for each one to complete the cycle you can then better prepare your business resources to service them. This enables you to minimise churn as well as manage cash flow. To analyse the effectiveness of your website and landing pages, obtain heatmaps and visitor recordings which are tools that enable you to see how visitors are interacting with the site and pages. This will equip you with data on where the holes lie and how you can improve the customer experience.

You need to be always working at it, and be prepared to adjust what you're doing based on your evaluations. Always test, always measure and always optimise.

SECTION 2

GO TO MARKET

Now that we've built our foundations, we can shift our focus to implementation. This will be more effective because you've taken the time to lay the building blocks, concrete the ground and put up the beams. Next, we build the rooms. In Sections Two and Three, I will take you through running marketing campaigns and marketing automation to achieve lead generation, lead qualifying, lead nurturing and customer retention.

Marketing automation is crucial here – you don't want to be doing things manually forever. If you want to scale, and I mean *really* scale, you're going to get busy and your focus needs to be on the right tasks. Marketing is great and very much necessary but it can be automated so that you can focus on growth.

One thing that's important to your growth is product innovation.

Never stop creating. Never stop evolving.

4

Lead Generation

As a startup, you may want to test market response. You may have a minimal viable product (MVP) and want to see if there's interest before you commit to more development costs and efforts. To do this quickly and accurately, you need to invest in a pay-per-click campaign for lead generation.

When we think of lead generation, the first thing that comes to mind is pay-per-click (PPC). PPC is mainly associated with Google AdWords but there are many other touchpoints that can be considered, including paid social advertising, which encompasses Facebook ads, LinkedIn Ads and all other social channels that run a PPC program, such as Twitter and Instagram.

The biggest benefit of PPC is that you can instantly appear on page one of Google and the social newsfeeds, so you instantly get visitors back to your website, from which leads tend to follow.

Pay-per-click marketing

Let's take a look at some PPC stats.

Search ads can increase brand awareness by 80%

Brand awareness is crucial for startups trying to cut through a competitive market and be seen as a thought leader in the space. Lead generation campaigns may bring you leads, but branding is what's going to help close deals. You want your ads to put out a positive, respectable and memorable message – one that is also educational and not necessarily focused on getting you a demo or meeting booked.

According to LinkedIn, the average prospect needs to see somewhere between seven and ten content pieces from you before they convert and become a customer. So when you create your ads, you need to provide content and offers that cater to all parts of the buyer journey, for example:

- Promoting eBooks, guides and webinars at the awareness phase of the journey, where the content focuses mainly on answering popular questions and solving pain points.

- Combining that with branded video content of you answering frequently asked questions. (This content would not require an opt-in and would primarily focus on engagement.)

- Promoting whitepapers, more webinars and buyer guides at the consideration phase of the journey, where the content mainly focuses on how your product helps to solve their problems.

- These can be run to a remarketing audience as well.

65% of b2b companies have acquired a customer through LinkedIn paid ads

If you're in the b2b space, I highly recommend making LinkedIn your main channel of focus. If you're in the b2c space, you should be looking at Facebook and Google AdWords. They are a lot cheaper than LinkedIn, but also the targeting metrics they offer cater more to a consumer than a business market.

I also recommend that b2b businesses find their audience on LinkedIn and then, once those cookies are collected, remarket to them on Facebook and Google. This is more cost-effective, and you'll end up targeting them on a different channel, where their mood, frame of mind and expectations are different and they may be more prone to making a final decision to buy.

Customers who see retargeted ads are 70% more likely to convert on your website

If you're running any type of PPC campaign, you should absolutely make remarketing your focus. Remember that research shows that customers will see anywhere from seven to ten pieces of content from you before they actually convert on your website.

Don't be worried about flooding them with your ads or your content. I know that's one concern that comes up frequently among my clients. They worry that they are annoying their prospects by flooding them with too much content or, in their words, 'spamming' – to which I say two things:

1. It's not 'spamming' if you're giving them value-adding content that focuses on topics that they are interested in. If anything, it's a positive brand experience and it will improve their brand recall.

2. Did you know that the average consumer is exposed to approximately 4,000 messages per day and is therefore capable of ignoring anything that's not relevant to them? They will convert as soon as they realise, 'Oh, actually I do need this.' So definitely run remarketing campaigns. And you can do that across all three platforms – Google, Facebook and LinkedIn.

I'm not going to give advice on how to write your ads (this was covered in Chapter 2, 'Clarify Your Message') or how to pick your audience (this was covered in Chapter 1, 'Nailing Your Niche'). Essentially, these are the two elements that will ensure your pay-per-click efforts are effective. Get these right and success should follow.

I will, however, let you know about one crucial step you can take to ensure your pay-per-click campaigns are always running well and you don't become complacent – and that is testing.

Testing and optimisation

Testing allows you to experiment with different audience types, creatives, messages and landing pages to determine what works best. Let's look at it in greater detail.

A/B testing

A/B testing is a simple methodology that involves testing two or more variations of an element, whether it be a webpage, landing page, ad creative or audience targeting, and seeing which works better. Once you have the winning element you then test something else. Keep testing and creating opportunities for your conversions to go up. Once you see results, increase budgets.

Testing your advertising

Here are some things that you should test when it comes to advertising:

- Test your audience targeting parameters – yes, you've nailed your niche, but there are many factors on platforms such as Facebook and LinkedIn that you can test to see where the sweet spot lies. Try testing your message among different age groups, sexes, locations and interests on Facebook or company growth percentages, company sizes and skills on LinkedIn.

- Test your ad creative – which message, heading, subheading, image or video resonates best with your target audience? Run tests and you'll know.

Landing pages

Use a tool such as Google Optimize to test different elements of your landing pages and see which ones convert better. Test headings, images, copy, price variations, social media engagement elements and authority elements, such as reviews and calls to action. But never test all at the same time. Simply run one test at a time for a minimum of three to four weeks, depending on how much web traffic you receive, and once you've declared a clear winner, move on to the next test. Google Optimize gives you an actual percentage of which one has the highest probability of winning so you can get an early idea.

And remember – always keep testing.

Testing – what not to test

Here are some things that don't make good tests.

Don't test platforms

Testing Google AdWords against Facebook ads against LinkedIn Ads is not an effective test, and I'll tell you why. If you've ever had the pleasure of analysing visitor behaviour data and source attribution data like I have, then you'll have realised that your customer is on multiple platforms. Yes, one could be resulting in a higher number of last attribution leads for you, meaning that it was the last platform they used before they decided to give you a chance, but all are responsible for that lead finally deciding to convert. Remember, it takes six to eight touches to generate a viable sales lead.

So, saying 'Facebook ads don't work as well as Google Ads' and switching it off will only result in fewer total conversions for you. You need to ensure you look at the holistic data and understand your customers' conversion paths before you decide against a particular platform.

Don't test content types

Content is king – more on this in the next chapter. But if you're promoting or sponsoring your content via social platforms, you may be considering testing different types of content, such as blogs versus webinars versus eBooks versus podcasts.

Here's why testing and then sticking to one type of content is not a good idea. Similar to platforms, your customer likes to consume different types of content. Sometimes they like to read, sometimes they like to listen in their car and sometimes they like to watch a webinar while eating their lunch. In the end, if you can cater to all of those senses and desires, you will come out on top. Being present across multiple media gives you a bigger reach in their minds and keeps you top of mind.

Before you scream out, 'How am I going to have enough time to produce all of this content while wearing all the other hats that a startup founder has to wear?' consider this. You can create just one thirty-minute webinar on a SaaS platform such as Zoom. Then you can use the recording of that webinar to create the following:

- Ten short-snippet, two-minute videos from the webinar, to be used as social media posts or ads – you can use any simple video editing software for this

- One eBook or three blogs from transcribing the
  webinar – you can use a SaaS platform like Otter
  to do this

Once you have these at your disposal, you can create
a content strategy and calendar around it. This much
content can last as long as eight weeks, so you've sud-
denly created and automated over two months' worth
of content that can work behind the scenes for you at
collecting leads while you focus on more important
things.

Automate to accumulate

Automate? Yes. Use a platform such as Hootsuite,
Monday, HubSpot or one of the hundreds out there
for this. They can help you schedule your social media posts as well as the following:

- Easily create landing pages that you can A/B
  test – without the need of a website developer.
  The costs you spend on an automation platform
  are still cheaper than what you would spend on a
  developer. Plus, you'll have total control of it.

- Create email templates from multiple beautiful
  designs. Use the above content in the copy for
  further lead nurturing.

- Create workflows that last as long as eight
  weeks so that your leads can be nurtured in

the background while you work. Leads that are nurtured result in a 20% increase in sales, according to DemandGen, and increase purchases by 47%, according to the Annuitas Group.

Search Engine Optimisation (SEO)

When done right, PPC can be highly effective for startups and generating that first batch of leads and customers. But it comes with a big cost that cannot be sustained over time. Though I highly recommend using it in the first few months of going to market, I also recommend you start implementing organic or referral campaigns that will bring you free traffic. These include Search Engine Optimisation (SEO) and content and social marketing. More on content and social marketing in Chapters 5 and 6. Here, let's take a look at SEO.

If you look at the research below from Brafton, you'll notice that SEO plays a big part in lead generation.

Research has shown the major role that SEO plays in lead generation. A survey of marketing professionals compared SEO, PPC and social media marketing strategies and cited the following results in terms of impact on lead generation goals:

- B2B marketers: 57% stated that SEO had the greatest impact on lead generation goals, 25% voted for PPC and 18% for social media

- B2C marketers: 41% claimed that SEO had the greatest impact, compared to 34% who found PPC the most influential, and 25% voted for social media

SEO is certainly a campaign that you want to run side-by-side with your PPC campaigns. Once you're optimised, you'll start to generate free traffic to your website and won't have to spend as much on media costs. We know SEO takes time and works better as a long-term strategy, but what can you do to accelerate your SEO efforts?

First, you want to make sure that your website is built on a secure platform as HTTPS. Since 2014, Google has advocated for HTTPS as opposed to HTTP sites, stating: 'We want to convince you that all communications should be secure by default.'

You also want to make sure your metadata is unique and relevant for each page. That includes your title, description and headers on the page (H1 to H3). If your website is built on WordPress, simply install the Yoast SEO plugin, which allows you to do this and get a score of how good it is for your target keyword.

Keywords are key

How do you get your target keyword? You want to use a keyword that's both relevant to your business and also trending. Type in some potential keywords related to your offering into a tool like Google Trends or AnswerThePublic to see all the conversational keywords that are trending around your offering, such as your why, what, where and how.

This provides you with a clear opportunity to see what your articles should be about. Name your articles after these keywords for optimum SEO results, and at the same time help answer your prospects' most frequently asked questions. Not the ones that you *think* should be featured on your website, but the real ones your customers have.

Bonus for you. These conversational keywords not only appeal more to your niche but they also allow you to be optimised for voice search. Voice search involves a person using Google Home or Alexa or that little microphone button in the search bar.

When people search with voice, they search differently. They don't say the words that they would normally type – they search as if they are asking a friend a question. For example, if you're looking for a property investing class, here's how you would search on each platform:

- **Typing:** 'Property investing class'
- **Talking:** 'Where can I find a property investing class?'

It's important to review your what, why, where and how searches and write content around them. It's a no-brainer when you consider that Search Engine Land released data that found nearly 50% of consumers are using voice for web searches.

So, now that you have the blueprint for finding what your customers want to read about or hear about, get to it my friend. Dedicate time each week to writing content. You'll be so happy you invested that time when, months down the track, your organic traffic is growing and sales are following.

Take care of the foundations

Do you have a xml sitemap and robots.txt file? A sitemap is an XML file which contains a list of all of the webpages on your site as well as metadata (the title and description of each page). Both a robots.txt file and a sitemap allow search engines to crawl through an index of all the webpages on your site in one place. Google loves you for it because you're essentially offering up a floorplan of your website without them having to go to your Open House blind, without knowing the size of your property (or amount of content on your website). See what I did there? We're back at that house analogy again.

Once you have these foundations right on your website, you can focus on content creation. The more content you create and the more you share it via social media platforms – with a link back to your website – the more traffic you'll obtain. You also give Google another reason to come over to your house and inspect the new rooms, to give you a better page rank.

Link building

Link building is another factor of SEO. It means that there is a link back to your website from another website. Google is supposed to love this because it sees it as a vote or advocacy.

But link building has become a dirty word. You see, many websites historically have used the services of dodgy link building companies to get as many links as possible to help with their SEO efforts. This usually consisted of low-traffic websites being created that just featured links, with no relevant or engaging content on them. Google has cracked down on this and has since penalised any website using these. Ouch! Try contacting that dodgy company to get your link removed. Not easy. I've had many clients coming to me with this problem and unfortunately there is not much I can do to help.

So, what's my recommendation on link building? Quality over quantity, my friend.

If you look at the first page of Google, it's populated with all the quality websites such as Wikipedia, LinkedIn, YouTube, Facebook, etc. My recommendation is to do your own link building by posting new and engaging content on your social media platforms, with a link back to your website in some of your posts.

You can also try to get your blogs or articles featured on popular magazine websites such as Forbes and Medium. These would make for fantastic links back. You can use a tool such as SourceBottle to help you do your own PR and get your articles out there to quality publishing sites. In their own words, SourceBottle is a free and easy-to-use connection platform that enables journalists and bloggers to efficiently find knowledgeable sources – sources such as yourself.

5

Social Marketing

In this chapter, I want to explore social media as a lead generation engine you should be using as you're gearing up to go to market. I will explore some more detailed techniques that you can be exploiting on each platform. I will predominantly focus on Facebook and LinkedIn paid and non-paid techniques that you can easily use yourself. This is where I have seen the greatest success for my clients, especially those who are getting ready to go to market. Let's start with the most popular one.

Utilising Facebook marketing

Facebook has close to 3 billion active users, so having a strong presence there is crucial to connecting with today's consumers, generating new leads and clients for your business, and bringing more awareness of your brand.

Regardless of your industry, your customer is on Facebook. The key is ensuring that your marketing strategy on this platform consistently grows your social media following, boosts engagement, and gets people to take action (for example, by clicking on your link or opting into your list).

If you follow all the principles in Section One of this book, you should have no issues in creating impeccable content and ad campaigns that run in the background to generate you leads.

Content is king! By sharing valuable posts that offer solutions, answer questions, and give helpful tips on Facebook, you'll position yourself and your brand as a thought leader and authority in your industry. Your content will compel people to join your list so they stay connected and in the know.

Grow like a pro

Content creation is great but it must have a purpose. The best way to make your content on social media work for you is to add a specific and targeted call to action to it. For example, if you're sharing an eBook or guide, collect an email address in return for it. Also, if you're sharing blog content, you'll want to encourage viewers to subscribe to your blog.

Yes, content helps with SEO and it also helps to position you as a thought leader, but you need the ability to grow your email list too, especially in the world of b2b marketing where, on average, it takes 84 days to convert 13% of your leads.

Hence, growing your email list is the lifeblood of your business. From this crucial foundation, you can convert new leads and boost revenue opportunities. But many businesses don't know how to go about it in the most effective way.

I like to relate it to a first date. Think of it like this. You've secured the first date and this is when the person will get their first impression of you. That is, unless they've already stalked you online, which is likely, whether you're securing a soulmate or a client. Either way, this is your chance to impress them. It's the same when a potential client first visits your website landing page – and the place where you're going to ask them for more details to nurture them towards a sale.

Most companies make the mistake of asking for too many contact fields. I don't have enough fingers and toes to count the number of times I've come across businesses asking for name, email, phone, job title, company name, company size and current provider from the get-go.

Would you do this on the first date? That's like sitting down for dinner and asking this person their income, their mother's maiden name, their first dog's name, the first street that they lived on. Seems a bit suss, no?

It's no wonder that these potential clients are not filling out these forms. And if that's you on the first date, it's no wonder you're not getting another. Sorry.

Keep it short and sweet. Less is more. Four contact fields is the new black. OK?

And remember this. Everybody knows that if people are going to opt in to your list and share their contact details with you, they need to receive something of value in return. With that in mind, I want to share with you six ways to effectively generate new leads on Facebook.

Six best practices on Facebook

1. Share expert advice that appeals to your niche

Publishing quality-rich content is at the centre of growing your business. Your blog posts, videos, email content, ads and social media posts are there to attract your ideal customer to your brand and, ultimately, to your list.

Your niche should guide your creation process for your Facebook content. Showcase your expertise by giving advice, tips, and tricks that your audience would find useful. Promote your blog posts, landing pages, and videos to boost awareness and add value.

2. Create a landing page especially for your Facebook followers

When people click on your link from your ad or Facebook post, your landing page content should speak to those followers. This will significantly increase conversions because it's targeted to that audience, and appeals to a solution they've expressed interest in. If the content offer on your landing page is congruent with the message you've promoted on Facebook, visitors are more likely to opt in.

An excellent lead magnet example to feature on your landing page would be an eBook or a video series that outlines the steps your customers need to take to solve their pain points.

Consider these other key pointers towards designing a winning landing page for your Facebook marketing:

- Highlight one offer per landing page to keep it hyper-focused.

- Use images and videos that complement the content to boost SEO and the user website experience.

- Have a clear call to action that gives direction on what to do next.

- Make landing pages actionable with content that goes deep into solving a problem.

- Target keyword phrases that your audience is actively searching for.

- Sell and demonstrate the benefits they'll receive from your content offer in return for opting into your list.

Remember, after you've built your first landing page, you must continually test variations to improve your conversion metrics and achieve maximum results. The best way to do that is with a tool like Google Optimize, which allows you to run A/B experiments on different variations of your landing page.

3. Ramp up your visual strategy

Statistics prove that adding visuals to your Facebook content raises engagement. Facebook posts with images receive 2.3 times more engagement than those without images, according to HubSpot. Additionally, Facebook users watch 8 billion videos per day. Investing in your visual strategy for your brand will drive huge attention to your content and open doors for obtaining fresh leads from social media.

Here are some tips for ramping up your visual strategy to bolster your lead generation from Facebook:

- **Use high-quality images** – The more photos you share that highlight the features and benefits of your products, the more interest you'll generate. Carousels and collages are great for showcasing many images.

- **Post social videos** – Video posts have 135% greater organic reach than photo posts on Facebook. Videos have a remarkable way of captivating viewers and moving people to action. Implement videos into your content strategy to create awareness and capture leads. Give the call to action during and at the end of the video, showing people where they can leverage your content offer.

- **Stream from Facebook Live** – One of the fastest ways to build your brand, Facebook Live is an extraordinary way to build trust with your followers while bringing more exposure to your business. Use a mixture of organic uploads and live videos in your Facebook marketing. Be sure to promote the time of your live broadcast in advance to boost viewership.

4. Use Facebook ads

A final tactic for generating new leads on Facebook is through paid ads. By running Facebook ad campaigns, you'll grow your followership, and increase lead and sales conversions. Facebook makes it easy to create targeted ads for your intended audience. They are also highly cost-effective and can fit any budget or goal.

Here are some recommendations for optimising your Facebook ads targeting:

- Consider narrowing the age range. Test a smaller range by choosing an age range of ten years, such as thirty to forty years old. This may help cut costs while still showing your ad primarily to your target audience.

- Leverage the 'Must also Match' feature to boost engagement and reduce costs by up to 25%. This allows you to go beyond choosing just a group of interests in your ad settings.

- Facebook retargeting is a must. Having your ad content follow visitors everywhere they go significantly boosts conversions and keeps your brand top of mind after people leave the platform. In all my years of running ads, I have seen that 'eight' tends to be the sweet spot. That is, an ad is typically seen eight times before a customer decides to convert.

- Create a lookalike audience of people who have already converted on your ads. Do this by uploading your customer list into Facebook and asking it to match people like them. With the amount of information people tend to share with Facebook, you'd be surprised how accurate and effective this is.

5. Create exclusive groups

Facebook groups are perfect platforms that allow you to build a community around your brand and keep like-minded people connected. By fostering conversations, you'll breed brand loyalty, encourage feedback from customers, and inspire users to engage with others. Groups also offer an opportunity for members to ask questions and get quick responses from you, which further humanises your brand.

Creating and maintaining an active social group will do wonders for your marketing. Sharing your quality-rich blog posts will provide value to your audience while driving traffic to your website, thus improving SEO ranking. Offering exclusive promotions and discounts to your group will elicit new and repeat sales.

6. Leverage influencers

Influencer marketing is a big hit and can catapult your presence online when done correctly. Building relationships with industry leaders will allow you to increase your brand awareness among their large audiences. But remember, it's a partnership... and it doesn't happen overnight. Influencer marketing must be done in a way that creates winning situations for everyone. When you approach influencers to set up a partnership, you have to approach them with the attitude, 'Here's how I can help you.'

One way to capture the attention of influencers is to regularly engage with their content. Like, comment, and share their content with due credit. In time, they'll begin to notice your involvement and will do the same for you, putting your name in front of their followers.

You can also consider tagging them in your posts, but be sure that you're offering value to their audiences in these, such as quotes and industry-related topics. Refrain from tagging influencers simply to promote your business or products. This is a big no-no and will make you appear spammy. Remain hopeful in your strategy of relationship building, as influencer marketing can lead to new opportunities and amazing collaborations.

Utilising LinkedIn marketing

OK, I may be biased here as LinkedIn just happens to be my favourite tool. Why? It's brought me immense success from comparably little effort. If you're in the b2b industry, this platform is an absolute must. Unlike Facebook, this is where people come to – and expect to – do business. They aren't on LinkedIn to connect with friends or share their lunch photos. They understand that this is a business platform and are more open to connecting with and absorbing content from strangers.

I usually recommend to my b2b clients that they find their niche on LinkedIn, because it has the parameters to give them that audience. I then recommend they remarket to that audience on Facebook, because we know they're also there and it's cheaper than LinkedIn.

Let's look at why LinkedIn is a social media platform you can't afford to ignore, along with the best strategies for maximising your results on there. The following statistics come directly from LinkedIn's own *Marketing Solutions Blog*:

- LinkedIn is the number one social media site for Fortune 500 companies.

- LinkedIn is, by far, better than any other social media site for generating leads; 80% of b2b leads from social media come from LinkedIn.

- Users are in positions of influence. More than 60 million LinkedIn users are senior-level influencers.

- 81% of b2b marketers use LinkedIn for product launches. It's the perfect platform for startups.

Leveraging LinkedIn

There are a few components to LinkedIn, each of them offering effective ways to engage with your audience on this site. These are:

- **Your profile** – Your LinkedIn profile is your central hub for presenting yourself to the world.

- **Your content** – I mentioned earlier the importance of content. On LinkedIn specifically, publishing articles lets you build your credibility, profile and thought leadership status. Use a tool like LinkedIn Pulse to share consistent content and position yourself as a thought leader in your industry and field.

- **Groups** – Joining or starting specific groups your intended audience follows lets you target your communications even further.

- **Paid ads** – There are several options for advertising on LinkedIn. My personal favourite is InMail Ads as they have on average a 50% open rate, which is significant when you compare it to email's 20% open rate.

- **Direct messaging** – Your ability to contact other members is the best way to grow your customer base. But don't go selling to them on first contact – you need to add value first. Drive traffic to your blog, website and other channels, where the lead magnets you have in place will help you capture contact details and further nurture your leads.

Let's look at these and other LinkedIn strategies in more detail.

Be a power profiler

LinkedIn reports that 50% of customers avoid people with incomplete profiles. In other words, even before there's any engagement, people are judging you based on your profile. When people see a profile that lacks depth and doesn't reveal much, they assume you haven't put much thought into it or, worse, that you don't have very impressive credentials.

Here are some tips for optimising your LinkedIn profile:

- **Use a quality headshot** – Your photo is one of the first things visitors to your profile will notice. Profiles with photos receive twenty-one times more profile views, which should be enough reason to visit a photographer's studio if you don't already have a suitable photo to post. Your photo should show you in appropriate attire for your industry and target audience.

- **Create a custom URL** – LinkedIn gives you the option to edit your default URL and change it to something more personalised. You can use your own name or your business name.

- **Optimise your headline** – Just as in emails and articles, profile headings are crucial for attracting attention and giving viewers an idea of what you have to offer. Industry-related keywords inserted into your headline also makes you easier to find in searches by your target audience. You have 120 characters for your headline, so use them wisely.

- **Make your summary stand out** – You have plenty of room to describe yourself in the summary – you can make it as long as 2,000 characters. While you should definitely take advantage of this space, be careful not to fill it up with jargon and buzzwords. Give your audience genuine insight into your product offering and why you're so passionate about it, as well as how it aims to change the world.

- **Upload media** – There's a section of your profile where you can upload media such as photos, videos and audio files. Take advantage of this and add some content that showcases some of your best content and accomplishments. Video and slides, preferably. This is also where your demo video of your product can go so that bottom-of-funnel users can access it easily. Make sure to include a call to action in your video.

- **Solicit recommendations and endorsements** – LinkedIn gives you a way to display social proof right on your profile. Ask colleagues, customers and anyone familiar with your work for testimonials. They can also endorse you for specific skills. Make it a habit to request testimonials and endorsements whenever you complete a project.

Personal branding versus company branding

When creating your profile and submitting content to LinkedIn, you have to decide whether to emphasise your personal brand or your business brand. For most small and midsize businesses, it's more beneficial to focus on your personal brand. What you're really doing on LinkedIn is building relationships. People want to engage with a person, not a company. That's why you should always have a photo of yourself as your profile photo rather than a business logo.

Unless you already have a high profile, it can be challenging to build a company brand. You're competing with thousands of companies with gigantic budgets and even substantial media coverage. Your business name and logo can easily get overlooked. As an individual, you have a chance to make an impression and stand out. Your experience, qualifications, and personality are uniquely yours. Be sure that this comes across in all your communications.

In another sense, personal and company branding are not mutually exclusive. When you build your own brand, you're also contributing to your company's image. Depending on the context, you might introduce yourself by saying, 'It's John from XYZ Solutions...' It's usually easier and more natural to introduce yourself first. This also lets you connect your LinkedIn content with everything else you put out, including your website, other social media content, blog posts, videos, podcasts or anything else you do.

Sales Navigator hacks and tips

Sales Navigator is a powerful LinkedIn tool for generating targeted leads. This is one of LinkedIn's premium services so it's not available with a free account. But if you use it, you'll probably find it pays for itself fairly quickly. You'll have the ability to send fifty InMail messages per month (or more, depending on which plan you choose). When you send a message to a prospect, they are likely to check out your profile and see what you've shared recently.

Here are some other hacks to help you get more than your money's worth from Sales Navigator.

- **Automate your efforts** – Want to connect with a large list of leads as quickly as possible and short on time? Automate it! Have a look at a tool such as OctopusCRM, which automates everything for you. You can connect with a specific list of leads you've identified and automate the sending of follow-up messages once they've accepted the connection. You can even endorse them for skills using this platform, which will help with building that relationship and generating a response from them.

I love introducing this tool to my clients because I get the funniest responses after they've used it. One in particular was: 'OMG, Octopus is my new best friend! I have just connected with 1,000 people and have booked nine demos in just one week! What the... ?'

That result would have previously taken that client a whole month to achieve. OMG indeed!

- **Get the most targeted leads** – One of the best features of Sales Navigator is that it gives you access to advanced search filters. You can pinpoint your searches based on geography, job title, company type and size, industry, and other criteria. Experiment with these to find out which settings provide you with the most promising leads.

  Other features can help you identify the most targeted leads, such as Sales Spotlight, which lets you know, at a glance, which companies are most likely to respond to you based on industry, whether they follow you on LinkedIn, and other considerations. There's also a 'view similar' button that lets you pull up leads similar to ones you've identified as highly targeted.

Another useful trick is to apply the TeamLink filter, which brings up warmer leads – those with whom you have a second-degree connection. With these, you can refer to your shared first-degree connections, who you could ask to provide an introduction.

Send compelling InMail messages

InMail is LinkedIn's internal messaging system. While the format is similar to sending an email, In-Mail has certain advantages. The majority of users (ie those with free accounts) can only send InMail to members they're already connected with. Not only do people get far less InMail than email but they're more likely to consider the former as coming from someone at least somewhat familiar and trustworthy.

At the same time, it's up to you to send messages that spark the reader's interest and that don't come across as intrusive, irrelevant, or spammy.

Don't attempt to automate the process by sending the exact same message to every prospect. Do enough research on each lead that you can mention something specific about them. For larger companies, you might search for recent news you can refer to. You might also comment on an article or link the lead has recently shared on LinkedIn.

Build relationships first

I also cannot emphasise enough the importance of building a relationship before you talk about your product. In the world of boxing, you would use a strategy known as 'Jab, Jab, Hook'. In your LinkedIn outreach strategy, the jabs are the warm-ups that help you build rapport with your target individual and the hook is when you hook them into your offer.

The first jab could sound something like this: 'Hi [first name], I saw that we both know [similar connection] and work in [industry] so thought it wouldn't be a terrible idea to reach out.'

The second jab, once they've connected with you, could sound something like this: 'Thanks for connecting, just curious what has been the single most influential technology that's helped you in your day-to-day?'

Keep these short and sweet and conversational. The idea is to get this individual to notice you and start a conversation with you. Once you feel like you've achieved your warm-up, you go in for the hook.

A hook could sound like this:

> 'Based on our conversation, I think you might find some great insight in this eBook/scorecard/whitepaper I put together. Here's a link to it. Would love to get your feedback on it.'

'Based on our conversation, I think you might get a kick out of this new technology I've created. Would love to give you a glimpse into it if you have a spare ten mins this Friday morning.'

Now here's a bad example of the kind of LinkedIn message I consistently receive from the get-go (before I have even connected with the individuals sending them).

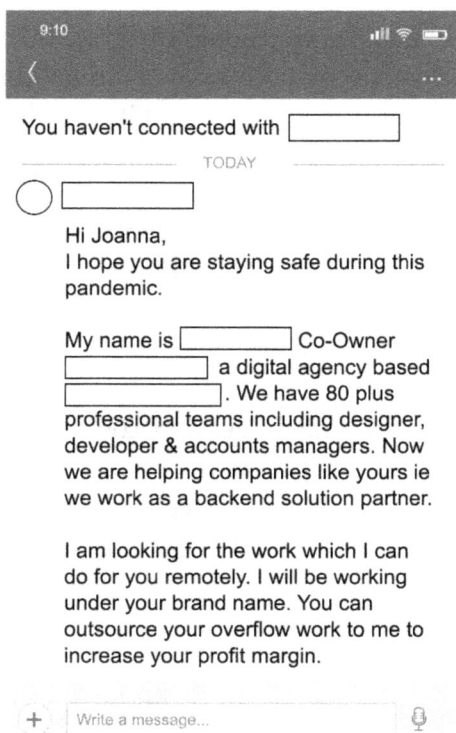

Sample LinkedIn message

I don't know anything about this individual and already they are trying to sell me something. That's an instant turn-off for me. You'll also notice that the copy is all about them:

- My name is…

- We have…

- We are helping…

- We are working as…

- I am looking for…

- I will be working…

If I related this scenario to a first date again, I'd say this guy is going in for a kiss but he hasn't even bought me dinner yet. Nor has he bothered to find out what I actually need/want/desire/struggle with – and he spelt my name wrong!

If he had just asked me those conversational questions first, he would have known exactly what to sell me and probably been successful at it.

Unfortunately, messages like this bad one are all too common on LinkedIn and I highly suggest you avoid doing it. It's not a numbers game. You're better off building relationships with fewer people and having quality conversations with them rather than sending a generic message to everyone. It just doesn't work.

For a truly custom approach to connecting with the right individuals and customising your message to them, you'll want to check out my chapter on account-based marketing (Chapter Eight).

Follow great examples

Let's look at some examples of personal and company accounts that are getting amazing results with LinkedIn:

- **Brian Hartzer** – Brian Hartzer, CEO of Westpac Group, made the top of the list for *Business Insider*'s Top LinkedIn Profiles in Australia. One feature of Hartzer's page that immediately stands out is that he strikes a good balance between promoting his company and his personal brand. He writes many articles himself and also shares relevant stories. He shares news items and articles about topical issues such as the importance of small businesses, the emergence of female leaders in banking, and the drought affecting NSW.

- **Hays** – Hays' company page was awarded LinkedIn's Best Company page (an award bestowed by LinkedIn itself) two years in a row. This global recruiting company excels in several areas with its LinkedIn marketing. They share lots of engaging content. The page provides people with useful information – some recent articles cover topics such as improving your listening skills, why coding is a valuable skill to learn, and addressing workplace loneliness. They also share content in a variety of formats including text, quality images, videos, and podcasts. Many of their ads allow prospects to download valuable reports such as a guide to creating a winning CV and salary guides targeted to specific regions.

- **Acciona** – Acciona is a company that specialises in infrastructure and renewable energy solutions. Involved in more than thirty countries, Acciona has recently been awarded contracts in Scotland and Australia. Acciona uses LinkedIn to build brand awareness among investors and opinion leaders concerned with energy. With its Business as Unusual campaign, the company found success by launching a series of educational videos to its LinkedIn audience. Acciona also partners with influencers to help make its message more accessible. In one video, for example, NBA star Marc Gasol helps to convey the urgency of investing in clean water and sustainable energy. With segmentation and content targeted to the interests of each audience, Acciona managed to acquire more than 1.2 million unique video views, with viewing and completion (the percentage of viewers who watch the entire video) rates well above industry averages.

Over to you

Whether you want to focus on your personal or company brand, LinkedIn is one of the best resources for reaching a wider audience of business decision makers. I've shared some of the best strategies for getting the most from your LinkedIn presence. But it's important to map out your own unique approach that showcases your best qualities. Make your profile complete and engaging and remember to keep adding to it and editing it as necessary. Publish content consistently. If you want to get even faster results, supplement these activities with paid advertising.

Consider the wise words of Oscar Wilde when putting yourself out there on LinkedIn: 'Be yourself; everyone else is taken.'

6

Content Marketing

Pay-per-click advertising and social media marketing are great tools for lead generation but they are much more effective when backed up by great content. Why is content important? Because content marketing costs 62% less than outbound marketing and generates three times as many leads, according to the Content Marketing Institute.

Lead generation via content marketing

Let's address the first goal of lead generation via content marketing. My greatest customer success case with this comes from none other than global tech giant Lenovo. Via content marketing, I helped them generate US$66 million in just twelve months.

This was a humongous campaign and there was certainly lots of advertising budget fuelling it. But by applying the same principles I did, you too can have reason to smile. Hopefully one day, 66 million reasons to smile.

Focus on people, not on brand

The most effective thing we did for Lenovo was to focus on the key people who worked at Lenovo, as opposed to the brand itself. When we wrote content, we added it to a brand agnostic educational website by the name of www.techrevolution.asia so people were more open to subscribing to it. The Lenovo logo was subtly added to the footer of each piece but it wasn't the focus by any means. We then assigned each blog to a key person in the sales and marketing department at Lenovo who was in charge of talking to potential customers.

Why was the focus on people, not brand? Because people are social beings and they love connecting with other people. They don't want to connect with a brand, they want to connect with a person. By connecting with a key person within an industry, they feel closer and therefore more likely to commit to a relationship with this person.

If you have someone who can be that face of the company – and I'm mainly looking at you here – then make sure all content comes from them. Position them (ie you) as the thought leader in your industry. Thought leadership is crucial to your content marketing success. More than 60% of C-suite executives said they were more willing to pay a premium to companies that create thought leadership content, while 45% of decision makers said they invited a producer of thought leadership content to bid on a project when they had not previously considered the organisation.

Keep in mind that your content needs to be educational and that you need to be adding value. By doing so, customers will naturally be drawn to you. You just have to trust the process and play the long game – although it takes time and consistency, it certainly delivers results. Remember the LinkedIn golden rule: it takes seven to ten pieces of content on average to close a customer.

Content creates inbound marketing

If customers see you as a thought leader or key person of influence in your industry as a result of your content, they will reach out to you. That's what we call inbound marketing. You don't have to sell, you just have to share knowledge and expertise on topics they're interested in.

One of the largest sales by a single salesperson in Lenovo during that twelve-month campaign was for US$3 million. The customer had called the salesperson in and had been amazed by all the content he had received from him. The salesperson was taken back and asked if it had been too much, to which the customer replied: 'I learned all there is to know about data-centres of the future from your content.'

Sale closed.

Don't feel like you need to limit your content to writing about your services and offering. Get a good understanding of your customers' pain points, in and outside of work, and write about those. Some of the top-performing articles that we wrote for Lenovo weren't even tech-related. They were about leadership, productivity and time management. Our target audience was the C-suite and we knew those were topics they were interested in, so that's how we got their attention.

Now what kind of content marketing should you be doing? Blogs and eBooks, definitely. Remember, the best way to research your topics is by looking at where your target audience is, what they are reading and what they are searching for. You can use tools such as BuzzSumo and AnswerThePublic to gauge trending topics as well as the most searched for keywords on Google.

This will help improve your engagement score with your target audience but will also help with your SEO. Content ranks well in Google, especially when people have engaged with it via social channels.

Webinar marketing

Webinars have absolutely exploded thanks to Covid-19. If you look at Google Trends data from December 2019, the trending score was 5 out of 100, which is extremely low. It basically means that few people were searching the keyword 'webinars'. If you look at the same data from three months later, March 2020, when social distancing and lockdown were strictly enforced, then you see a score of 100 out of 100 which is the highest rank you can possibly get.

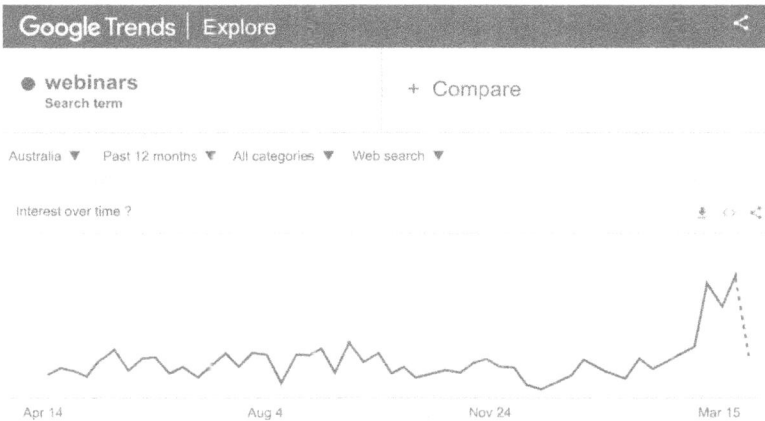

Google Trends Report for 'Webinars' (Google Trends report © 2020 Google)

A lot of businesses realised then that webinars are crucial to their survival. But they are a medium that they should have jumped on long ago. If you're not doing webinar marketing right now, you're definitely falling behind your competitors.

Webinars are crucial for SaaS or any startup that needs to visually explain what their product does. They are also crucial if your target audience is made up of the C-suite, a common audience at Hat Media, as they are extremely time-poor. They may have little time to read an eBook, but they are happy to sit back and watch a webinar in their downtime or while on the road.

There's a catch with webinars, though. If you consider where they sit in the marketing funnel, you will find most companies using them at the bottom of the funnel. This is a big mistake. I see lots of SaaS companies using webinars to showcase their software – many of their audience lose interest then because they aren't ready for a demo yet. That should come afterwards.

A webinar, similar to an eBook, should focus on solving the customer's key pain points. That way, it's worth their time watching it and exchanging their contact information with you to do so. You can then spend the last five minutes of the webinar touching on how your product can solve these pain points and offering them to sign up to a free demo.

Plan with your customer in mind

When promoting a webinar, keep your campaign short. My recommendation is two to three weeks. 59%

of registrations for webinars happen in the last week leading up to the webinar and 33% on the day of the webinar itself. So don't feel like this is something you need to plan out months in advance. Your customers won't want to wait long for an event they've just signed up for, or they'll lose interest and completely forget about it or find content somewhere else that offers an on-demand option.

Another thing to note is that a third of registrants only ever watch the webinar replay and 51% of on-demand views happen during the fourteen days after the webinar. So don't expect big attendance numbers or numerous deals from one webinar. It's crucial that you record your webinar and make it on-demand so that more people can watch it while you focus on other things.

You should also create a lead nurture campaign for your webinar. Using a marketing automation platform, you can continue to nurture your webinar registrants via email, to invite them to future webinars or to view other bits of content that you've created. At some point in your nurture strategy, you should start to include case studies and customer success stories to help you bring them further down the marketing funnel and close the sale.

Let's now look at the ways in which content marketing and marketing automation can help with lead qualification and lead nurturing.

Lead qualification via content marketing

How do we get higher quality leads? This is a vital question for startups in the b2b space. I've said this before, but it's an important factor to note so I'll say it again: if you're in the b2b space, I highly recommend you make LinkedIn your main focus and your new best friend.

We've already looked at the benefits of LinkedIn for targeting exactly who you want. But aside from cherry-picking your audience, there's another Linked-In hack you can use to help capture customer details.

As you know, when you're offering a content piece to a customer such as an eBook, webinar or blog subscription, the key objective is to collect their contact information so that you can continue to nurture them and then eventually close the deal. You also know that once you get them on your content landing page, you don't want to be asking too many questions on the form field, because they'll just get overwhelmed and jump off.

So, when providing a content asset, you're usually asking for a name, email and perhaps one or two more fields. But you might then spend an obscene amount of time later trying to figure out if they are a qualified lead. Here's a cool shortcut to obtaining that information quicker.

On your forms, add an 'Autofill with LinkedIn' button. This enables customers to prefill all details by simply logging in to their LinkedIn account. It's a simple two-click process for them and it provides you with all their historical career data you want to know, such as job title, company name, size of organisation, etc. Easy!

If you're using a marketing automation platform, you can also add the 'LinkedIn Bio' field to the forms and gain lots of information about your leads that way. Based on this info, you can put automation in place that segments qualified leads from non-qualified ones to focus your lead nurturing tactics on the right people.

Lead nurturing via content marketing

So, you've captured many leads using all of the tips in my last few chapters. What's next? Nurturing them, of course!

Leads that are effectively nurtured produce a 20% increase in sales. Also, effective lead nurturing generates 50% more sales-ready leads at a 33% lower cost.

How do you nurture leads?

The obvious action is to feed them to your marketing automation platform and send them a series of emails that add value and keep your brand top of mind. (More on marketing automation in the next chapter.)

Here's a list of email workflows you should be creating for your leads and your existing customers for up-sell opportunities. Triggers here refers to how you initially obtained the contacts' email address. This is important to know and segment as it will allow you to create a more personalised workflow depending on the type of content or media they consumed:

1. **Topic workflows** – Main triggers: page views or content offer downloads

2. **Blog subscriber welcome workflow** – Main trigger: subscription to your blog

3. **New customer welcome/training workflow** – Main trigger: lifecycle stage

4. **Upsell workflow** – Main trigger: past purchases

While sending these is somewhat effective, it's also what everybody else is doing. Here's my recommendation on how to stand out.

Don't just nurture them through emails – nurture them via LinkedIn InMails as well. Unlike regular email, which has a 20% open rate on average, InMails get an average open rate of 60%. You'll be more than doubling the visibility of your message.

But remember, don't send everyone the exact same InMail message. Your InMails need their own content strategy. They need to be shorter and more personalised. You'll be sending them via your personal LinkedIn profile, so make sure to add a human touch to them. Send no more than three or four messages, otherwise that's considered spamming. Unlike email, they should be kept to a minimum and the frequency should be fortnightly to monthly. You don't want to scare away your lead by triggering constant LinkedIn notifications.

The idea is to remain a thought leader and to continue to add value. Trust the process and the customer will come to you.

SECTION 3

DOMINATE THE MARKET

O K, guys, despite what the name of this book tells you, I don't want you to simply go to market. I want you to dominate this thing! Dominate the industry you play in and give your competitors something to cry about.

If you take the time to do the homework from the first section on building your foundation and implement consistent and ongoing pay-per-click, social media and content marketing strategies and campaigns, you'll see lots of new leads and customers signing up. So much so that you will start to experience growing pains – pains like:

- Keeping up with the demand that new leads and customers bring

- Finding ways to improve and align your marketing and sales efforts

- Dealing with customer complaints and requests

But for each of these pains, I can help you:

- Keep up with increased demand without having to invest so much in additional labour costs – hello, 'Marketing Automation' (Chapter Seven)

- Improve and align your marketing and sales efforts and focus on recruiting whales of new clients instead of just fish – hello, 'Account-Based Marketing' (Chapter Eight)

- Minimise churn and instead turn customers into your biggest advocates – hello, 'Customer Retention Strategies' (Chapter Nine)

7

Marketing Automation

How awesome would it be if in the future we could all clone ourselves and achieve so much more with our time? Oh, wait… the future is now and your clone has a name. It's called HubSpot, or Pardot, or Eloqua, or any other tool that gives you marketing automation capabilities.

Whether you're a startup or an established business, you likely have the following four goals in mind:

1. Lead generation
2. Lead qualifying
3. Lead nurturing
4. Customer retention

Marketing automation allows you to achieve these goals in a quicker and easier way so you work smart, not hard. I'll focus on the ways you can do this in this chapter, but first, let's look at some more reasons why you should be using marketing automation.

Why use marketing automation?

First, according to Forrester, spending on marketing automation tools is forecast to grow rapidly, reaching $25.1 billion annually by 2023. You certainly want to be part of this game if you are to not just survive but thrive in the digital world we live in.

Second, you should know that your consumers have by now grown accustomed to rapid and hyper-personalised information at their fingertips. Marketing automation is expected by your customers. Consumers are demanding relevant experiences from the brands they interact with. They expect brands to know their likes and preferences, and come up with intelligent product recommendations that are worth their while.

As more businesses have scaled up their digital-based campaigns on market trends and global impact, the role of automation has become crucial in keeping the momentum going. The purpose of marketing automation, ultimately, is to allow for tailored messages to go out with consistency, rather than applying manual effort. Customers still feel like messages are personalised to them, rather than getting a generic message, but there are fewer chances of error, since that communication can go out automatically at a scheduled time.

Finally, let me share some benefits of effective marketing automation:

- Businesses using marketing automation to nurture prospects see a 451% increase in qualified leads, according to the Annuitas Group.

- Sales productivity increases by 14.5% while marketing overheads are reduced by 12.2%, according to Nucleus Research.

- The biggest benefit reported of course is 'less time wasted', which leaves you to do other, more important things with your time.

So, how do you make marketing automation truly effective? What are some of the best practices needed to ensure that your marketing is targeted and helps nurture and grow your customer base? Let's take a look.

Marketing automation best practice

Maintain your contact database

When you first start your automation efforts, you're probably starting with clean data. Everyone is contactable, emails aren't bouncing, click/open rates remain solid... and then there's a bit of a drop-off. All of a sudden, your numbers go down, and you aren't totally sure why. The possible culprit? A not-so-clean database. The truth is, people move around a lot, they change jobs, they get a new email address – nothing is ever static. To ensure your database continues to yield good results, it's important to schedule periodic cleanouts. Set a bi-annual, quarterly, or whatever other time frame suits you best to sift through your database and give the data a spring clean.

Remember it's not always about promotion

One of the key points that businesses always fail to recognise is that marketing automation isn't *just* about marketing. It's about providing value, creating a narrative and connecting to your customer base. When scheduling and planning emails, try to sprinkle in non-promotional content. Look at your content scheduled and think about the following questions:

- Does it add value?

- Does it provide resources?

- Do I ask for feedback/thoughts/ideas?

- Am I showing the best of what we have?

Ideally, your marketing automation content calendar should have something that addresses at least three of these questions. This way, you can balance promotional material with resourceful and helpful information that will encourage readers to open your emails.

Dive deep into the buying cycle

Your content won't be much use if you aren't aligned with customer behaviour, so it's time to take a data deep dive. Look at your site user data and try to understand:

- How long it takes for customers from putting something in their cart to buying it

- How many pages on your site they visit in between

- How many times they come to, exit and come back to your site before purchasing

- When your website seems to get the most and least overall traffic

It's like detective work, but these are all important questions to help you create a buyer timeline and create content accordingly. If you know customers take about a month from discovering your site to asking for more information and/or a demo, you can create helpful introductory content to your product. If you start to see a pattern where there is an enquiry for more information but the purchase takes another two to three months, you can build content that could help them towards making that decision (ie case studies, FAQs, etc).

Marketing automation strategies

Marketing automation is about creating a strategy rooted in personalisation and efficiency. Through these best practices, you can establish a solid foundation for your overall marketing and continue to build on it. As you deploy campaigns and get more data back, you can continue to tweak your automation efforts to better match customer behaviour and habits, making it even more effective.

Once you have your marketing automation strategy and blueprint, it's really just about careful implementation so that it works for you behind the scenes in the best way. Instead of writing you a step-by-step course of how to create this implementation, I encourage you to look at my online course instead, where you'll find video examples of how to use a platform like HubSpot to implement automation. Not using HubSpot? Don't worry. In my opinion, once you know one platform, you know them all. I created these videos to give you the strategy that you can apply to any platform. For more information, go to my website www.hatmedia.com.au.

8

Account-based Marketing

I've put this chapter under 'Dominate the Market' as I see it as a second step, for once you're already established with a few good customer success stories on board and you've clearly identified the future customers you want.

Account-based marketing is not a good strategy to go to market, but it's the best strategy to scale and grow and dominate the market.

What is account-based marketing?

Account-based marketing (ABM) has the power to transform the way you attract large clients to partner with you. More than 87% of marketers believe ABM has a higher ROI than other marketing efforts, while 85% believe it's more successful for retaining current customers. But that's only true if it's done right. Miss the mark, and the consequences could be devastating. If you focus on a few large accounts, losing even one of them could spell doom for your revenue and growth projections.

To prevent that worst-case scenario, it pays to be strategic. A focus on the right tactics and clients is only the beginning. In this chapter, I'll explore best practices that can elevate your account-based marketing and help to ensure its success for both short- and long-term business growth. Let's begin.

Identify accounts and contacts

As in any other type of marketing, the best ABM strategies begin with your audience. Knowing exactly who to target is the crucial first step in ensuring the success of your messaging and promotional efforts.

The following are some Ideal Client Profile (ICP) questions you need to answer to identify the people you want to invest time on:

- Which pain points does your solution aim to solve?

- Which organisations and potential clients have actively told you about and exhibited these pain points?

- What size company are you looking to attract?

- What do you know about the number of companies at that size in your industry?

- What do you know about your competitors in that space, including their (and your) current market share?

- Can you identify individual leads among your target accounts that can serve as your entry into their organisation?

You can probably answer the first five without help. That last piece, though, requires at least some research. It's not always easy to know who the stakeholders, gatekeepers and buying agents in your target accounts are.

That's where tools like LinkedIn Sales Navigator enter the equation. Advanced lead search enables you to find not just target accounts, but the right contacts within those accounts. Customised lead suggestions provide a clearer picture, while CRM integrations allow you to record contact data for follow-ups. Finally, a live feed of activities by these contacts helps you stay up-to-date and make your connection more relevant to them.

Listen to track accounts

Part of building that lead profile includes knowing what your audience does and wants to talk about.

That, in turn, requires a unique version of the social listening component that has become so beneficial for marketers across industries. Listening to key stakeholders within individual accounts for lead nurturing purposes is a crucial next step.

Lead nurturing is a core part of almost any type of digital marketing campaign, but it takes centre-stage when the individual account becomes the focus. I find that the sales cycle, in this case, will be significantly shorter if the lead is nurtured correctly.

In social listening parameters, marketers track conversations around their brand and industry. In account-based marketing, the same concept applies to tracking the conversations, mentions, and posts of the specific leads you're communicating with and trying to convert. The people to focus on here are the stakeholders who would have a formal or informal role in any contract you're trying to sign with your prospective customer.

More specifically, you're monitoring for a few key pieces of information:

- Conversations in online groups and on social media – these give insight into your prospects' areas of interest in the industry

- Original posts on social media – these provide a better idea of the types of topics your prospects are most passionate about

- News alerts about your individual prospects – these allow you to better understand their current work and accolades, and give you a natural 'in' as a conversation starter

A number of tools can help you monitor these types of activity. Some, like Tweetdeck, are free but relatively limited. Others, like Brandwatch, are more comprehensive in providing actionable insights across platforms but also tend to be more complex and will cost a monthly fee.

Crucially, listening is not just monitoring. It means taking the information and making it actionable, 'responding' with the hyper-personalised content we outlined above. That's why platforms like Brandwatch, which categorise conversations, tend to be beneficial as they build more comprehensive reports that can form the basis of future communication.

You must follow up diligently with relevant information and ongoing support. It's not enough to simply send a few updates about your company and hope for the sale. Your emails need to be customised to each lead's needs and pain points. Avoid direct selling messages and instead focus on building value. Above all, the emails should seem like they're coming directly from you, the representative of your company, not a random 'no-reply' email address.

Finally, the messages should reach your contacts where they spend their time, which (in most b2b scenarios) is a mix of both email and social media. Two tools will become especially helpful as you nurture your leads with these types of personal messages:

1. **HubSpot email** – This helps you build automated email flows without losing that much-needed personal touch. You can build visual email templates that are designed to generate high open and reply rates. You can also track your analytics to better understand which types of nurturing emails your prospects respond to, and which fall on deaf ears.

2. **LinkedIn InMail** – This is a more customised tool but also more personal. LinkedIn's internal messaging platform is more comprehensive than those on other social networks. You have the ability to send sponsored InMails that stay at the top of your prospect's inbox for up to forty-five days. InMail also benefits from a less crowded environment, in that it doesn't have to compete with the numerous other emails the average businessperson receives every week.

Hyper-personalise content

You might think that because ABM mostly applies to a b2b environment, it should be strictly rational.

But that's not necessarily true. Studies have repeatedly found that b2b buyers are just as, if not even more, emotionally invested than their consumer counterparts. That, in turn, opens the door to hyper-personalising and storytelling opportunities. By hyper-personalising and telling stories with your messaging, there is a greater likelihood that your content will be remembered and shared, and that your key leads will resonate with it.

What is hyper-personalised content marketing?

Hyper-personalised content marketing leverages real-time data and artificial intelligence to provide consumers with more relevant information about the goods and products your business provides.

Personalisation focuses on standard, transactional consumer information, such as their name, organisation, position within their organisation, and purchase history. Hyper-personalisation entails more detailed information, such as behavioural and real-time data, which can be used to create highly relevant material for users.

For example, you can look at the history of a prospect's activity on LinkedIn to find out what topics they have engaged with and what groups they are part of to design content that you know will resonate with them.

A hyper-personalisation framework consists of four components:

- **Data collection** – This is the most essential element for creating a highly functional framework, as it enables you to not only identify who your customers are, but also their wants and needs. While businesses of all sizes can benefit from data collection, it is especially beneficial for firms that service a wide variety of consumers. This is because the more diverse your customer base is, the more difficult it can be to provide them with the most relevant marketing material for them.

- **Customer segmentation** – This refers to the process of separating consumers into groups based on similar characteristics, such as their demographic, location, website activity, purchase history, and so on. Segmentation makes it easy for firms to interact with each diverse group efficiently and appropriately, via hyper-personalised communications.

- **Targeted journeys** – After data has been collected and your customers have been segmented, you need to choose the best time to make contact with them and ensure the communications they are receiving are in line with their wants and needs.

- **Measurement and analysis** – This step is meant as a means of fine-tuning previous targeted campaigns. The idea behind measurement and analysis is to gain a more comprehensive understanding of the metrics that have a profound impact on your bottom line. Once you're clear about the techniques that work, you can then replicate proven tactics and improve any inefficiencies to help boost conversion rates and grow revenue.

What are the benefits of hyper-personalisation?

Some benefits of hyper-personalisation for prospects as well as existing customers include:

- **More relevant marketing material** – As stated above, one of the benefits of hyper-personalisation is that it allows firms to create highly relevant marketing material for prospects in search of the goods and services your business provides. It means less time, effort and money wasted producing content.

- **Enhanced buyer experiences** – Highly relevant marketing materials enable businesses to provide content that facilitates the customer's purchasing process, which enhances efficiency and the overall customer experience.

- **Increased customer loyalty** – When you enhance your customer's experience by providing a streamlined purchasing process for them, you create positive emotion in them. Their positive interactions with your brand boost customer retention and loyalty.

In today's competitive market, it's difficult to capture the attention of consumers with intent. Using ABM techniques like hyper-personalisation can assist in the acquisition of high-quality leads, which translate into higher conversion rates and an increase in company revenue.

Hyper-personalised content and ABM

We know that using an ABM content strategy can help you reach your targets faster, and that the key to ABM is building and nurturing relationships with your individual prospects and contacts. This is especially powerful when you don't just state plain facts and data about why they should partner with you, but weave those facts into a larger narrative that's easy for your audience to follow.

Case studies are the most obvious examples of storytelling in b2b. They take hypothetical benefits and make them come to life through real-world application examples. But case studies are far from your only storytelling opportunity in this medium.

As you personalise your content, consider how you can give it the traditional story arc:

- **The problem** – The moment when the audience realises that they have a problem and tries to find a solution

- **The struggle** – The time when the audience tries to solve its problems but faces significant adversity that it has to overcome

- **The resolution** – The climax, when the audience finds that crucial thing that makes the story come to a happy end

Through this structure, you can capture your audience's attention, and keep it through to the final resolution – which is, of course, your company. Case studies can follow that concept, but so can anything from an email to a single post on LinkedIn. Building a story means engaging your prospects' emotions, which makes them more likely to pay attention and ultimately become your customers.

Implementing hyper-personalised content

This starts with narrowing down the above-mentioned pain points to the specific situation in which your prospects would benefit from your software. Build content, from individual nurturing messages to entire case studies and whitepapers, specifically addressed towards these.

According to Gartner, organisations who personalise their digital marketing outsell those who don't by more than 30%. But it's not just about inserting some dynamic content or substituting in a prospect's first name in an email. Hyper-personalisation is:

- Data-driven, based on visitor and account data to deliver content specifically designed for that audience

- Predictive, based on data points that suggest and predict intent to increase relevance to the customer

- Interactive, allowing the recipient to customise their experience to their liking

It's not easy to hit on all three of these points, but it's far from impossible. Put simply, it requires a unique marketing strategy for every account, and even every lead you're trying to target.

That starts with data. Learn as much as possible about every lead in your database, from their professional background to the nuances of their current position and how they would be involved in a potential part-nership with your company. Connect that lead data back to the larger account data to build context and to see the bigger picture.

From there, the process is similar to that of creating buyer personas. Except, in this case, you are building profiles of actual human beings. These profiles then become your content guides. They offer a foundation for brainstorming potential topics, and a resource to ensure you create your content specifically for the outlined needs and wants. Your hyper-personalised content pieces can then be distributed via your lead nurturing channels.

Consider the power of multi-origin messaging

You will likely encounter your prospects on more than one channel, and the more channels you can reach them through, the better. But you might not be aware that the sender of the message is just as powerful as the message itself. Switching senders can give out a powerful message to your prospects. If ABM is true one-to-one marketing, chances are your prospects won't react well to a message coming from a faceless corporate account. The same is true if their only point of contact is a salesperson.

ABM provides an opportunity to vary the sender and build a complex nurturing stream. In the course of that stream, your prospects may receive messages from the sales team, a customer success specialist, and a member of the C-suite relevant to them. That will increase trust, and build a feeling of being wanted on your contacts' side.

Of course, and once again, this type of strategy is complex and requires significant time to both plan and execute. You'll need to answer a few core questions:

- Who would your prospects most like to hear from?

- What types of messages might be relevant from those specific senders?

- Can you guarantee that, should a lead seek out the sender via a reply or indirectly, that sender would be both responsive and consistent in their messaging?

The answers to these questions will make a multi-sender campaign extremely powerful. They'll also allow you to stay within reason, incorporating only individuals within your company that are actually relevant to your prospects. The result is a more comprehensive, more sweeping campaign designed to capture, and keep, your prospects' attention.

Target the right niche

As marketers and business owners, we use different types of content to reach a wide audience at various stages in our sales funnel. With ABM, you 'flip the funnel', and deliver personalised messages to your top targets rather than casting a wide net.

The benefit of this content strategy for ABM is that account-specific messaging leads to higher revenues in less time. Your target clients are also less likely to glaze over reading your message because it's all about them.

Let's take a look at how ABM and content strategy work together to help you achieve your sales goals.

How to integrate content strategy with ABM

First, select highly qualified accounts that fit perfectly into your target market. The top accounts you want to go after will depend on a number of factors, including industry, location, company size or annual revenue, and even company culture. Then you create an ideal customer profile that goes deeper than your buyer personas.

Next, the content strategy comes in. You'll have identified the ideal customer's 'pain points', which your company is uniquely equipped to solve. What is your unique value proposition for each account? Creating content to address these pain points is where you begin developing content marketing strategy in step with your ABM.

Now you can set to work creating custom content that meets the accounts and their decision makers right where they are. Rather than having to churn out generic content that will reach people at various stages in the funnel or increase search rankings, ABM content strategy takes the most valuable prospects and speaks right to them. This goes a step beyond personalising content.

Planning and creating ABM content

To plan ABM content, you need to focus on three things: content operations, a tiered approach, and a content framework. This makes sure everyone in all departments is on the same page and your efforts are defined.

Examples of ABM content marketing might mean you:

- Create personalised landing pages on your website for each account

- Mention your top accounts on social media and in blog posts

- Offer free tools targeted to your selected decision makers

- Use retargeting tools to provide content that will move your decision makers closer to a sale

- Use your decision makers' email addresses to create a custom list for sending a targeted message or for targeted advertising

- Send a personalised email to a decision maker from a real email address at your company – not through email marketing software

When it comes to creating content for your target, see if you can revamp content you've already invested time, money, and effort into. Editing and personalising existing content that speaks to a decision maker can make your ABM content marketing strategy less taxing on your resources.

Automating and measuring ABM content

You can create content for a handful of your top accounts, not just one account at a time, if it's relevant of course. Some companies scale and automate their ABM content to be more efficient for even more accounts. But some marketers would say that isn't true ABM – just regular funnel marketing. You can decide for yourself if that is a strategy you'd like to implement.

It's important to measure the results of your content. How effective is it? Analyse the engagement, downloads, and clicks. Retarget your top accounts with additional, more finely tuned content to move them closer to conversion.

Strategy breeds success

ABM has the potential to be immensely powerful – if you can get it right. As you have seen, it requires nuances and tactics that are different from typical marketing efforts, especially when it comes to hyper-personalisation and listening to your key stakeholders.

But with these best practices, your ABM strategy will be poised for success. Your messages will be more nuanced, more complex, and more relevant. You'll maximise their chances of getting through to your audience and converting more high-quality prospects into long-term clients, which will sustain and support your growth strategies.

9

Customer Retention

Every business, big or small, should care about customer retention. Here's why: retaining your existing clients is significantly cheaper than acquiring new ones, while also bringing in bigger revenues. In other words, its ROI is significant. One study found that increasing your retention rate by just 5% can improve your revenue by up to 95%.

Existing customers already know about you. They have already taken the biggest leap by engaging with you to begin with. Convincing them to stay on, upgrade, or work with you again will take less effort – if you know how to do it.

Improving customer retention via customer service

1. Create a customer community on social media

We touched on Facebook and LinkedIn groups in previous chapters. These are great platforms to use and invite existing customers to. They create a community and members can help each other out if they stumble upon an issue with your product. We call this user-generated content and it absolutely helps to relieve you from providing customer support.

Because you know what your existing clients love even more than hearing from you? Hearing from their peers. After all, there is a reason that 84% of internet users trust online reviews from complete strangers as much as personal recommendations from their friends.

A representative from your business should be involved as the admin of this group and to moderate the content in case it really gets out of hand, but they should not be the driving force. The goal is to provide an authentic mechanism for your audience to help each other.

Facebook and LinkedIn both offer group features that can help you build this type of community. Between the two, Facebook tends to be the better choice because of its larger user group, but LinkedIn could make sense for more business-oriented industries.

One great example of this is when we launched a private Facebook group for QSN Health. As they aim to help smokers quit smoking, the goal was to invite customers so that they could share their quitting journeys with each other. Here's what happened when this community started to grow:

- User-generated stories started to form around how effective QSN's product was, and how it had few side effects compared to what else was on the market.

- If one person complained about something like slow shipping, for example, the other users quickly jumped on to defend the brand.

- Some users were scared the product wouldn't work for them and they were quickly reassured and inspired by those it had worked for, who were now feeling more positive about their journey.

- Best of all was when customers started to invite their friends to the group, who then ended up buying the product based on the stories they saw there. Kerching!

2. Offer exclusive content and tutorials

Don't underestimate your customers' appreciation for content that goes above and beyond what they expect. In addition to the services or products they pay for, provide additional content that is only accessible for your current customers. The result will be greater engagement with your brand, and a greater chance of contract renewal or repeat purchase.

The reason why this type of exclusive content works is based on a scientific concept. The reciprocity principle states that if we receive something for free, we will feel compelled to return the favour. It's the same concept that prompts retailers to offer free food samples. Through webinars, product tutorials, and more, you can make your mark in your customers' minds and improve your retention rates.

When customer retention strategies are implemented right, via the use of email, social media, and content marketing, then you'll better retain your existing customers and maximise your revenue. The result is healthier and more sustainable business growth, which increases your ROI and improves your bottom line.

Let's now explore the ways we can automate customer retention strategies.

Improving customer retention via automation

1. Build retention workflows

You should already be using marketing automation to nurture new leads. But did you know that you can use the same technology to improve your retention as well?

The basics are simple: set up a starting condition, along with a number of emails that are specifically designed to ensure a positive customer experience. Over time, you can use these emails to gently nudge your customers to buy from you again.

For example, you may set up an initial email that introduces a new client to your service shortly after the contract is signed. From that point forward, regular emails can go out that lets the now-existing client know how the relationship is structured, and how you can partner further together in the future. These emails should always place value at the forefront, only subtly mentioning potential upsell possibilities.

Depending on your business model, retention workflows can start at any point. For some brands, it might make sense to get started as soon as a lead becomes a customer. For others, particularly businesses with longer average customer lifetimes, a better strategy might be to set up an initial wait condition and only begin the re-nurturing process once existing customers start to become inactive.

2. Check in after each customer service

Each time a customer contacts your company for service, no doubt you do your best to provide a quick and satisfying solution. But not all problems are solved immediately, first time around. From packages damaged in shipping to online account problems, it's always best to check in with your customers after a solution has been implemented to ensure they are satisfied.

Automated marketing tools can do that by sending a friendly check-in message to customers three to twelve hours after they have contacted customer service. Show you care by ensuring customers are satisfied with a follow-up for each and every service. This also gives you a chance to get reviews and feedback.

3. Email customers when their complaints result in improvements

This will be beneficial to SaaS startups specifically. It's common to get a series of website bug reports and customer service complaints. Most of these are repeats or the customer misunderstanding your interface. But sometimes, a customer's report reveals a real problem that needs fixing or a flaw in your business design that can be turned into a serious improvement.

When this happens, keep your customers in the loop. Use automated marketing tools to personally acknowledge and thank each customer who reports a problem that you then fix. This has two benefits. One, you let them know that their previous complaint has been resolved. Two, your customers feel personally involved as a contributing part of the brand family, not just another purchase number.

4. Cross-sell and upsell

When you begin to implement automated cross- and upselling, the one principle to always remember is this: market in the customer's best interests. Do your best to develop your automation and UI so that customers are shown content that would improve their experience, not just increase their revenue spent with you.

Help customers compare features, prices, and reviews quickly. Help them identify when there's a better-performing product, or show them supplies or add-ons required for a product to be enjoyed. Use your cross-selling automation powers for good, and your customers will remember and respect you for it.

Similarly, upselling should be a gentle process. Automated marketing allows you to display better products and highlight how they are better, while still giving the customers the opportunity to choose.

Take Amazon's comparison chart for many products on the platform. It compares the relative features of up to four similar products. This allows customers to judge for themselves whether there's something better and, essentially, to upsell themselves.

The benefits of customer retention are far and wide and shouldn't be ignored. Not only are customers the lifeline of your business, they also allow you to obtain greater learnings in your field of expertise and can become your biggest advocates. The overall benefits include:

- Cheaper customer acquisition

- Upsell and cross-sell opportunities

- Enablement of a referral system

- Building advocacy and creation of customer success stories

SECTION 4

BEYOND THE MARKET

Congratulations! This section is designed to help you once you've gone to market and had great success. If this is you and you can finally relax after all that blood, sweat, and tears that have gone into launching your startup, then I commend you. Not many startups get to this stage.

But I know you. You have an entrepreneurial spirit. You can't sit in your comfort zone for too long and you're likely plotting the ways you can evolve further. Two things that will help you immensely are covered in this section. They are:

- Keeping up with innovations (Chapter 10)

- Going global (Chapter 11)

These elements are the next step in your entrepreneurial journey and I shall guide you through them. They are the only two ways in which you can scale beyond what you already have. But they require caution. They require patience.

In the next two chapters, I'll cover the importance of innovation – the idea being that you must keep innovating or you will fall behind – and the risk factors of going global and what you need to consider before you attempt it.

Get these right and you will have success beyond your wildest dreams. You will also be one of few, so it will truly be a great achievement.

10

Keeping Up With Innovations

Innovation is the reason why I'm where I am today. At the peak of my career in digital marketing, when I started my own company back in 2008, Facebook was only two years old and not well-known. My company was primarily offering Google AdWords, SEO and website services and many businesses were still advertising in the Yellow Pages and had to be convinced that online is where it's at.

I know many competitors/businesses that stuck to these services only and ended up closing shop because clients learned that they could easily be done in-house or outsourced to someone cheaper.

Luckily for me, I am all for innovation and quickly jumped on the next wave of marketing innovations such as social media marketing and inbound marketing.

As a result of embracing these new campaigns, I landed my first enterprise inbound marketing client, not just for Australia but the entire Asia Pacific, by the name of Lenovo. Having a case study to add to the company name quickly made us popular with other enterprise clients and we ended up doing content marketing for of some of the greatest tech enterprises in Australia. This meant an explosion in revenue and the ability to triple the in-house team and the number of suppliers.

The need for innovation is the most crucial step to your foundation. Remember, back at 'Nailing Your Niche', it wasn't just about realising your niche and message once – you need to keep doing this as you evolve.

If you are to thrive as a business, it's imperative that you keep up with the latest innovations in your industry. Do this and you will start to attract a new type of customer. This calls for a revisit of all the things we've discussed up to now. For your new niche, you'll need a new message and buyer journey map.

The importance of innovation

Innovation is key to maintaining your digital standing, growing your market share, and securing your place as a stalwart of the digital business ecosystem. The following dives into the importance of innovation for digital businesses, what happens if you lose sight of innovation as a business goal, and what innovations you should prioritise over the next year.

Innovation is the disruptor of every industry. It turns things upside down and reshuffles the balance of power. Embracing innovation is instrumental to ensuring that your business remains sustainable and healthy over the long-term. There are several reasons for this.

Innovation excites top talent

According to IBM, 42% of millennials and 47% of Gen Xers have stated they would leave their current job for a 'more innovative environment'.

The best employees want to work for the best companies. These highly skilled individuals are attracted to organisations that strive to produce the best for all their stakeholders – not just their customers. By investing in top innovations, your business can highlight that you want to provide unparalleled services and goods to customers, as well as illustrating that you want the workforce to be equipped with best-in-class tools and systems. It is this type of mindset that creates a strong workforce culture, where co-workers inspire the best in one another and magnetically pull in a dream team.

If you've had experience with poor-performing employees (and I know I've had my fair share), you'll know just how important this is. Finding those talented gems is hard and retaining them is even harder. By keeping up with innovation and giving them challenges and new software to learn, they will stay excited and feel like they are progressing.

Innovation excites customers

Customers are more demanding than ever before. They know what they want, when they want it, and how they want it, and they are vocal about it. The truth is, there is enough competition and technology is advancing at such a rapid rate that any given customer preference, wish, or desire can be met after a little bit of research and development.

Having a customer-first mindset is paramount to innovation. In a PwC study that focused on the six characteristics of superior innovators, researchers found that gathering deep customer insights is the most valuable capability for developing innovative ideas.

The companies that opt for meeting customer preferences by integrating smart innovations will reap the rewards. They will expand their customer base and reduce customer attrition. They'll become linked with strong innovations which will, in turn, reflect positively on the brand.

Innovation differentiates one business from another

It seems like a new competitor jumps onto the scene every day. They offer something slightly different, slightly cheaper, or slightly something else. To stand out in all this white noise and capture your customer's attention, you need to be different – and in a good way. Implementing interesting and exciting innovations is the most effective method for accomplishing this. As long as your innovations improve upon your product, service, or operations in a way that is visible to the customer, you'll be on the right track.

Innovation allows businesses to scale

According to the same PwC study, the companies that are best at leveraging innovation see a sales growth that is more than two times higher than 90% of the world's 1,000 most innovative companies – so they're the best of the best.

Innovation, when implemented correctly, leads to growth. This is because the goal of any given innovation is to improve on something in a significant way. This could be automating a time-consuming task, more effectively identifying customer needs with artificial intelligence, or adding an element to a product or service that makes it more reliable. All of these improvements make it easier for a business to scale what they do, which leads to growth in profits and business capacity. In short, innovation allows businesses to reach their potential faster – much faster.

Innovation solves problems

Innovation allows companies to solve the various problems they face.

Is lagging delivery times angering customers? Give drones a try. Hey, it worked for Amazon! In fact, Amazon Prime Air is a service that will deliver packages weighing up to five pounds in thirty minutes or less using small drones. Is a fabric that your product contains too flimsy? Try a newly designed synthetic alternative that lasts year after year. Is your HR overwhelmed with the number of regulations they have to keep up with? Integrate one of the new RegTech applications that automate all compliance demands in any given business.

If your company is facing a bottleneck or pain point, there is an innovation that can remedy it. You just have to find it – it's simply one search away.

What happens when businesses fail to innovate?

What happens to a business when it decides to stick with the status quo and stay comfortable? If the customers are happy with the product and business is running smoothly, is it really that big of a deal to skip innovation and opt for business as usual? Unfortunately, it can turn into a big deal. All it takes is an agile startup to introduce itself to the industry or a successful company in an adjacent industry to invest in a little horizontal growth, or even a competitor to get inspired and reinvent itself.

In 1955, *Fortune* magazine created an infamous list, the Fortune 500. Every year, the 500 largest and most profitable companies made the list. But growth, being big, or making money are not signs of long-term stability and success. Proof of that can be seen by the fact that out of that inaugural list of 500 companies, only sixty still exist.

We can all think of companies where a failure to innovate was core to their downfall. From Blockbuster to Toys R Us, from Kodak to Yahoo, Segway, JCPenney, MySpace – the list goes on and on. Many of the companies were simply resting on their laurels, believing that no business model could possibly be better than theirs. Blockbuster is a great example of this. The company clung tightly to their in-store business model, stating that customers preferred the experience of coming to the store, with the possibility of seeing their friends and acquaintances and holding their rental choices in their hands as they walked around browsing the latest releases and old classics. Netflix proved this theory wrong.

What innovations should digital businesses embrace in 2021 and beyond?

The problem that many digital businesses face is choosing the right innovations to invest in. There are so many that it can be a challenge to pick out the right options and nearly impossible to keep up with the never-ending and ever-quickening release of innovations. To help lessen this burden, here are a few innovations that every digital company should prioritise over the coming year.

1. Mobile technology

This refers to 'mobile' in every sense of the word. It means equipping the workforce with mobile phones and tablets that enable them to do the work they need to do, when and where they need to do it. It also means understanding that customers, clients, and partners will want to connect with the company through their mobile devices and creating the mobile spaces to meet this demand.

Let's face it, mobile technology has completely taken over desktop. Looking at worldwide data, we see the trend.

2. Business intelligence tools

Cloud-based technology has changed the data landscape for businesses of every size. It has made data aggregation, analysis, and insight available to SMBs and SMEs alike. Digital businesses must take advantage of these intelligence tools, as they will provide them with a deeper look at everything from workforce productivity to customer buying patterns.

3. Chatbots

Chatbots are the perfect example of innovation being leveraged to save time and money, as well as meeting customer demands. They are an inexpensive solution that augment customer service with artificial intelligence, answer basic customer questions and allow customers to avoid the hassle of calling or emailing. This also allows customer service representatives to dedicate themselves to the more complex customer queries. Plus, chatbots don't have to sleep, so they're available any time of day or night.

4. Machine learning

Machine learning and blockchain are thought of as technologies that can only be used by the largest businesses, who have the capacity to build proofs of concept customised to their own systems and processes. This is no longer the case. For any business that collects data in significant amounts, machine learning can be used to predict customer behaviour and trends. With the number of out-of-box machine learning tools now available, any digital business can simply plug and play.

5. Cybersecurity

Digital businesses need to start investing in machine learning and blockchain for cybersecurity purposes. While blockchain provides cryptography to protect private data, as well as an unalterable record of all information, machine learning tools not only predict attacks, but also help to protect against them.

Choose your innovation

When it comes down to it, innovation is what makes a business thrive. It allows a company to perform better, both in terms of productivity and customer expectations. The companies that choose to harness the power of innovation will feel the benefits – all they need to do is pick the right innovations to invest in.

The tools I have invested in for the benefit of my businesses include:

- Dropbox
- HubSpot
- Salesforce/Pardot
- Eloqua
- SEMrush
- Canva
- Shutterstock
- Mailchimp
- Freshdesk
- Xero
- OptinMonster
- WooRank
- Moz
- Verblio
- Connectio.io
- Asana
- Teamwork
- OctopusCRM
- Analytics tools
- Programmatic tools

I could go on, but I've just named my favourite ones for three reasons:

1. They offer value for money.

2. They are easy to use and teach.

3. They make my life so much easier and free up my time.

11

Going Global

Why should a startup do business beyond Australia's borders? Why not!

Audience expansion is perhaps the most obvious reason. Australia's 25 million residents are served by just over 2 million small and medium-sized businesses, leading to an environment that's often crowded.

Expand overseas, and the pool of potential customers (and the resulting revenue) expands exponentially. This also has a positive impact on reputation. An impressive client portfolio is important for attracting both local and international clients. The power of social proof lends instant credibility to businesses as they are able to show success that isn't limited by borders.

Finally, going global enables startups to access a wider range of talent. Especially for SaaS businesses, talent is the biggest source of capital. But in any industry, the technology involved needs guidance and expertise to become a distinguishing factor for their business model. Any country into which your business expands opens new possibilities for talent acquisition to improve your human resources.

Risk factors

Despite the advantages mentioned above, going global does not guarantee success. A number of risk factors and disadvantages may well discourage you from taking this step in the first place. Each of them deserves further consideration.

According to a recent survey, only 10% of executives believe that their business has what it takes to succeed in a global market. Management thought leader IMD points out the strategy-execution gap as a major cause. Setting the right strategy is vital as other businesses lead the way. (We'll dive into that below.) Executing that strategy, however, remains challenging. The gap that can arise between what is planned and what actually happens causes both struggles and potential long-term failures for many businesses.

Generally speaking, going global is a risk in its own right. You're leaving your home market, with which you're familiar, in favour of other opportunities with a greater degree of uncertainty. The new environment may have significant differences, from laws and regulations to the business culture, and of course, the audience to whom you're marketing may in itself be a major change to what your company is used to and optimised for.

Factors affecting success or failure

With all of the above in mind, a picture emerges of the complexities that arise when going global. It pays to better understand the factors that will affect your business's success or failure when taking this step, such as:

- **The competitiveness of your home industry** – If you have significant growth potential within Australia, focusing your resources there may be the better investment, rather than withdrawing them in favour of foreign markets.

- **Global opportunity** – Are your products or services highly sought-after in markets overseas? How well is that niche already served? Look for markets you can enter without immediately having to contend with a crowded competitive environment.

- **Culture of expansion** – How well does your product, service, and business mission align with the cultures of the markets into which you plan to expand? How much training and retraining would your workforce need to make those adjustments?

- **Technological capabilities** – Digital businesses especially need to be conscious of this factor, given how much their business depends on it. Can your systems adjust easily to the new market?

- **Resource availability** – Entering a new market requires a large amount of work. You need to put in both human and capital resources to build brand awareness and the entire value chain. Having those resources available is a vital first step.

- **Embracing new (but different) opportunities** – Finally, the current company culture is a crucial consideration in taking this step. Your leadership and entire workforce need to embrace the ability to go global, and work hard to make that happen.

Each of these factors, on its own, can make or break your success. Get them right, and you have a good chance of overcoming the risks and building your business up substantially. Get any of them wrong, and you could cause significant damage to your business both immediately and long-term.

Five steps for going global

It's time to consider more closely the exact steps you should take to leverage the benefits and avoid the disadvantages of going global. This five-step formula is generally accepted as best practice – of course, your exact process may differ based on your unique situation and the competitive environment in which you operate.

1. Evaluate your capabilities

First things first, based on the above factors, you have to make sure that your startup actually has the capability to go global based on its current situation. That sounds like a simple step, but might be the most complex of them all. Evaluating your capabilities requires a thorough analysis of your local business situation, company culture, and more. In other words, you need to build a complete picture of your firm to allow you to form an educated opinion on whether going global is even a possibility.

2. Unearth market opportunities

Once you have a better idea of your startup's capabilities, it's time to start evaluating potential markets. No firm outside of the Fortune 500 will ever go truly global. Your best chance at success is finding a few key markets overseas and homing in on them for targeted growth. Expansion to further markets can come later.

Now your market analysis should focus on the industry you're operating in. Evaluate the competitive environment, and highlight the core value propositions and competencies of the players with whom you'd be competing. Then build a perceptual map to determine whether your own value proposition overlaps with existing offerings or occupies a gap, which would suggest a market need.

3. Determine market variables

If you do find overseas markets with specific opportunities, dig deeper into the variables that might determine the success and failure of your global operations. These include the culture, legal, and regulatory environment you're entering.

Even the largest corporations can fail at this stage. American supermarket giant Walmart had to exit Germany because its culture did not accept this type of business model. Australian companies like NAB and Bunnings suffered the same fate when trying to expand into the United Kingdom. A lack of understanding of these variables may cause you to fail, regardless of business size.

4. Ensure technology proficiency

Even if you find the right market for your capabilities, the journey is not done. Next comes the process of making sure that your technology is up to par in the global marketplace. Whether your business has major digital components or builds its entire business model on technology, chances are that without checking your technological proficiency, you are probably unprepared for what awaits you beyond Australian borders.

Again, this test can take on many shapes. You might need to make sure that your servers are powerful enough to handle global audiences, or account for time zone differences in your customer service. You might even run into bandwidth limitations in countries like China or India. Not considering these factors ahead of time might spell failure.

5. Test the market for potential opportunities

Finally, it's time to test the market. Remember, finding the right expansion opportunity does not guarantee success. You might have overlooked some nuances – though some are impossible to find before you step into this process. Testing the market will limit your risks as you begin to execute your expansion.

Some of that market testing should include advertising designed to build brand awareness and equity. Digital marketing is invaluable to determine how global audiences are responding to your efforts and offerings.

When faced with adversity, you can do one of two things as a startup: you can either allow it to overwhelm and consume you, or you can pivot and use it to your advantage. Trends that have grown in recent years can help startups reach more people and build more followers and customers. All it takes is ingenuity and a willingness to embrace change.

Summary

We've covered a lot of ground in this book and I've tried to give you as much practical advice as I possibly can to help you not just go to market, but succeed and grow beyond that.

All of the campaigns and strategies I have mentioned in this book have been tried, tested, and implemented multiple times for my own business, and for the hundreds of clients I have worked with over my fifteen-year career in the digital marketing space.

I know they work. All you have to do is put in the work and trust the process. You may not be able to do all of this yourself, so consider building yourself a dedicated and reliable team who can take on some of the responsibility. Alternatively, you can use an agency such as Hat Media to help out where needed. Many of our startup clients engage us to help them with launch and then train their internal team to keep it up and continue performing well.

My hope for you is that you take your product to market and see immense success. There's nothing I love more than seeing the little, innovative guys taking on the big fish and succeeding. They create more opportunities and innovations in the world and truly make it a better place.

Don't be overwhelmed by all the work that needs to go into your go-to-market strategies and campaigns either. Yes, it can be time-consuming at the start, but once you start to scale and gain some financial freedom, you should be able to get some work/life balance too. I'll never forget the days when I launched my startup agency and the blood, sweat, tears and night work that went into growing it. I'm sure if I had read more books at that time, I would have found success easier and quicker, but I don't regret anything for a minute.

I'm so happy to be where I am today. Owning a successful agency that does amazing and rewarding work for inspiring clients and the fact that I'm still able to pick my kids up from school every day and spend some time with them has made me truly happy in my career life. I wholeheartedly wish the same happiness for you.

Good luck, my friend, and remember – the smarter you work, the more luck you have!

What's next?

If you're feeling inspired by what you've learned and want to see visual and practical examples of how to put it into action, I invite you to explore my online course which is designed to give startups a leg up in determining their exact niche, building out their marketing funnel and going to market. Find it on my website: www.hatmedia.com.au

If you want to speak to me personally about your go-to-market strategy, I'm happy to have a consultation with you to make sure you're on the right track. Simply connect with me on LinkedIn: www.linkedin.com/in/joanainch

Acknowledgements

When I first decided to write this book, I had a specific goal in mind. I wanted to help the startup founders that wake up with stars in their eyes and passion in their blood every single day. They get to work on their amazing ideas that are capable of changing our world and truly making it a better place.

I've had the absolute and utmost pleasure in working directly with, or interviewing as part of my SaaS Stories series, a number of founders that are truly making a difference in the world. They are either changing the world of medicine and its accessibility or enabling small-time farmers who have difficulty with corruption and transparency to sell their crops to mid-buyers who believe in fair trade. They are changing the ways in which we work remotely or creating amazing AI capabilities within supply chains to help us be the best humans in the workplace that we can possibly be.

I work with a wide range of startups primarily in the technology and SaaS industries and my mind is blown each time I meet their founders and hear their stories. These amazing people truly inspire me and make me see the beauty of our world as well as all the innovative opportunities within it.

This book is for them. Specifically for those that are just getting started on their journey and cannot afford marketing agencies or big media budgets to get their word out and truly grow. I hope this book brings them the tools and the blueprint they need to get started and go to market so that their amazing idea can enlighten us all.

Thank you.

References

Acciona, 'Acciona wins €400m energy-from-waste contract in Scotland', *Biomass Magazine*, 2019, http://biomassmagazine com/articles/16410/acciona-wins-undefined400m-energy-from-waste-contract-in-scotland, accessed 1 October 2020

Adobe Marketo Engage, 'Calculating the REAL ROI from lead nurturing', 2015, https://uk.marketo.com/ebooks/calculating-the-roi-of-lead-nurturing, accessed 1 October 2020

Bernazzani, Sophia, 'Customer loyalty: The ultimate guide', Hubspot.com, no date, https://blog.hubspot.com/service/customer-loyalty, accessed 1 October 2020

Chaffey, Dave, 'Global social media research summary July 2020', Smart Insights, 2020, www. smartinsights.com/social-media-marketing/social-media-strategy/new-global-social-media-research, accessed 1 October 2020

Doerr, John, *Measure What Matters* (Portfolio, 2018)

Elkin, Noah, 'The long and winding road to real-time marketing', Gartner, 2017, https://blogs.gartner. com/noah-elkin/the-long-and-winding-road-to-real-time-marketing, accessed 1 October 2020

Fleming, Jane, 'Emotion in B2B buying: The evidence', LinkedIn.com, 2019, https://business. linkedin.com/en-uk/marketing-solutions/blog/ posts/content-marketing/2019/Emotion_in_B2B_ buying, accessed 1 October 2020

Gallant, Josh, '50+ LinkedIn statistics for 2020', Foundation Inc, 2020, https://foundationinc.co/lab/ b2b-marketing-linkedin-stats, accessed 1 October 2020

Gallo, Amy, 'The value of keeping the right customers', *Harvard Business Review,* 2014, https:// hbr.org/2014/10/the-value-of-keeping-the-right-customers, accessed 1 October 2020

Gomes, Ellen, 'Introducing the definitive guide to account-based marketing', Adobe Marketo Engage, 2017, https://blog.marketo.com/2017/03/

introducing-the-definitive-guide-to-account-based-marketing.html, accessed 1 October 2020

Heller Baird, Carolyn, 'Myths, exaggerations and uncomfortable truths: The real story behind Millennials in the workplace', IBM, 2015, www.ibm.com/downloads/cas/Q3ZVGRLP, accessed 1 October 2020

Hisaka, Alex, 'How B2B buyers perceive sales professionals', LinkedIn Sales Blog, 2014, www.linkedin.com/business/sales/blog/guides/how-b2b-buyers-perceive-sales-professionals, accessed 1 October 2020

Holiday, Ryan, *The Obstacle is the Way* (Portfolio, 2014)

Jaruzelski, Barry, 'Global innovation 1000: The six characteristics of superior innovators', PwC, 2018, www.digitalpulse.pwc.com.au/report-global-innovation-1000-study, accessed 1 October 2020

Lam, Bao and Verma, Koppel, 'New research shows search ads drive brand awareness', think with Google, 2014, www.thinkwithgoogle.com/_qs/documents/106/search-ads-drive-brand-awareness_articles.pdf, accessed 1 October 2020

Margugio, Gabriel, 'History of inbound marketing: Then and now', Nextiny Marketing, 2019, https://blog.nextinymarketing.com/history-of-inbound-marketing-then-and-now, accessed 1 October 2020

Mawhinney, Jesse, '50 visual content marketing statistics you should know in 2020', HubSpot, 2020, https://blog.HubSpot.com/marketing/visual-content-marketing-strategy, accessed 1 October 2020

McCoy, Julia, '9 stats that will make you want to invest in content marketing', Content Marketing Institute, 2017, https://contentmarketinginstitute.com/2017/10/stats-invest-content-marketing, accessed 1 October 2020

Meloni, Joe, 'Study: SEO better than PPC for lead generation', Brafton, 2011, www.brafton.com/news/study-seo-better-than-ppc-for-lead-generation, accessed 1 October 2020

Menyo, Jane, 'Wrap your head around ABM with these 24 statistics', ON24, 2019, www.on24.com/blog/24-statistics-to-wrap-your-head-around-abm, accessed 1 October 2020

Miller, Donald, *Building a StoryBrand* (Thomas Nelson, 2017)

'Mobile vs desktop internet usage (latest 2020 data)', Broadband Search, 2020, www.broadbandsearch.net/blog/mobile-desktop-internet-usage-statistics, accessed 1 October 2020

Murphy, Rosie, 'Local consumer review survey', BrightLocal, 2019, www.brightlocal.com/research/local-consumer-review-survey, accessed 1 October 2020

Musk, Elon, 'The mission of Tesla', Tesla website, 2013, www.tesla.com/en_GB/blog/mission-tesla, accessed 1 October 2020

Newton, Erik, 'HTTP vs HTTPS and SEO in 2019', Brightedge, no date, www.brightedge.com/blog/http-https-and-seo, accessed 1 October 2020

Pash, Chris, 'The top LinkedIn profiles in Australia for 2013', *Business Insider Australia*, 2018, www.businessinsider.com.au/the-top-linkedin-profiles-in-australia-for-2018-2018-11, accessed 1 October 2020

Pearson, Bryan, 'German lessons: What Walmart could have learned from Lidl, and vice versa', *Forbes*, 2018, www.forbes.com/sites/bryanpearson/2018/02/05/german-lessons-what-walmart-could-have-learned-from-lidl-and-vice-versa, accessed 1 October 2020

Perry, Mark, 'Fortune 500 Firms 1955 v. 2017', aei.org, 2017, www.aei.org/carpe-diem/fortune-500-firms-1955-v-2017-only-12-remain-thanks-to-the-creative-destruction-that-fuels-economic-prosperity, accessed 1 October 2020

Price, Penry, '7 surprising stats about the underappreciated power of thought leadership', LinkedIn Marketing Solutions Blog, 2018, https://business.linkedin.com/marketing-solutions/blog/linkedin-news/2018/7-surprising-stats-about-the-underappreciated-power-of-thought-l, accessed 1 October 2020

Raichshtain, Gilad, 'B2B Sales benchmark research finds some pipeline surprises', Salesforce.com, 2014, www.salesforce.com/blog/2014/11/b2b-sales-benchmark-research-finds-some-pipeline-surprises-infographic-gp.html, accessed 1 October 2020

Ross, Aaron and Lemkin, Jason, *From Impossible to Inevitable: How SaaS and other hyper-growth companies create predictable revenue* (Wiley, 2019)

Ruffolo, Bob, 'Lead nurturing: The ultimate guide for digital marketers [process and resources]', Impact, 2020, www.impactbnd.com/blog/what-is-lead-nurturing, accessed 1 October 2020

Rynne, Alex, 'LinkedIn content marketing tactical plan', LinkedIn Marketing Solutions, 2020, https://business.linkedin.com/marketing-solutions/content-marketing/linkedin-content-marketing-tactical-plan, accessed 1 October 2020

Savage, Jonathan, 'Top 5 Facebook video statistics for 2016', Social Media Today, 2016, www.socialmediatoday.com/marketing/top-5-facebook-video-statistics-2016-infographic, accessed 1 October 2020

Scandalios, Jenna, 'Extend the life and reach of your webinar with on demand', BrightTALK, 2015, https://business.brighttalk.com/blog/extend-the-life-and-reach-of-your-webinar-with-on-demand-html, accessed 1 October 2020

Simpson, Jon, 'Finding brand success in the digital world', *Forbes*, 2017. www.forbes.com/sites/forbesagencycouncil/2017/08/25/finding-brand-success-in-the-digital-world/?sh=a61522b626e2, accessed 1 October 2020

Spila, Dmytro, 'The process and performance of ad retargeting, and why you should be using it', Social Media Today, 2019, www.socialmediatoday.com/news/the-process-and-performance-of-ad-retargeting-and-why-you-should-be-using/568480, accessed 1 October 2020

Sterling, Greg, 'Nine voice search stats to close out 2019', Search Engine Land, 2019, https://searchengineland.com/nine-voice-search-stats-to-close-out-2019-326884, accessed 1 October 2020

Sweeney, Erica, 'Forrester: Marketing automation spend will reach $25B by 2023', Marketing Dive, 2018, www.marketingdive.com/news/forrester-marketing-automation-spend-will-reach-25b-by-2023/522900, accessed 1 October 2020

Tiffany, Amber, '10 webinar benchmarks every marketer should know', GoToWebinar, 2019, https://blog.gotomeeting.com/7-webinar-benchmarks-every-marketer-should-know, accessed 1 October 2020

Turpin, Dominique, Narasimhan, Anand and Cording, Margaret, 'Challenges in going global: 3 areas where companies struggle overseas, IMD, 2016, www.imd.org/research-knowledge/articles/challenges-in-going-global, accessed 1 October 2020

Wilcox, AJ, 'How to analyze your LinkedIn Ad performance', Social Media Examiner, 2020, www.socialmediaexaminer.com/how-to-analyze-linkedin-ad-performance, accessed 1 October 2020

The Author

Joana Inch has dedicated fifteen years to the digital marketing space, ten of which have been spent as the founder of digital marketing agency Hat Media, based in Manly Beach, Sydney, Australia.

Her true passion lies in the tech and SaaS space, helping enterprise clients and startups alike cut through, scale and grow with new and innovative digital strategies.

She runs regular events and webinars on selling SaaS and marketing automation for Microsoft for startups, and has launched an online learning course to help young startups gear up to go to market.

Want to chat? Find her on
in www.linkedin.com/in/joanainch

www.ingramcontent.com/pod-product-compliance
Lightning Source LLC
Chambersburg PA
CBHW071552200326
41519CB00021BB/6710